G000152609

Vegetarian
SOCIETY

Thank you to the following people, who helped make this book possible:

Lance Bell, Vicky Birch, Kate Bottomley, Simon Bromley, Antony Byatt, Alex Connell,
Fay Counts, Graham Drummond, Jen Elford, Lynne Elliot, Rose Elliot MBE, Alison Fawkner,
Susan Furmage, Julia Godridge, Susan Hardy, Diana Hawdon, Zoe Henderson, Rob Hobson,
Steven House, Geoff Lloyd, Denise Renshaw, Coral Sirett, Jonathan Smith, John Soonaye,
Julian Tait, Su Taylor, Daria Wawrzynska, Helen Watson, Laura Woodall.

Copyright © 2016 by the Vegetarian Society of the United Kingdom Ltd.

Reprinted January 2017.

The moral rights of the author have been asserted.

All rights reserved. No part of this publication may be reproduced, distributed, or transmitted in
any form or by any means, including photocopying, recording, or other electronic or mechanical
methods, without the prior written permission of the publisher, except in the case of brief
quotations embodied in critical reviews and certain other non-commercial uses permitted by
copyright law. For permission requests, write to the publisher at the address below:

The Vegetarian Society,
Parkdale, Dunham Road, Altrincham, WA14 4QG

Tel: 0161 925 2000
Email: info@vegsoc.org

www.vegsoc.org

ISBN: 978-0-900774-11-9

All photographs copyright © 2016 the Vegetarian Society of the United Kingdom Ltd except on
pages 18, 53, 66 (top), 130, 131 and 134

Printed in the United Kingdom

Registered Charity No. 259358 (England & Wales).
Registered Company No. 00959115 (England & Wales).

Happy,
Healthy and
Delicious

by

Vegetarian
SOCIETY

Vegetarian
SOCIETY

Contents

Desserts and Sweet Treats   126

Index   140

Notes   143

Foreword by Rose Elliot MBE

I'm tempted to call this the 'no more excuses' cook book: if ever you've wanted to go veggie but not quite managed it for one reason or another, then this is the book for you. Whatever got in the way before – not enough time? No ideas for tempting meals? Worried about not getting the right nutrients? Well, they're all covered here. All you have to do is enjoy cooking and eating the results! And with such easy and delicious recipes, that will be a pleasure.

Nearly all the recipes are pictured in colour, too, and that makes meal planning fun, and easy. So now really is the time to take the plunge – just do it! Keep some basic veggie ingredients in stock, have fun trying out one veggie meal, and then another, and another, one day at a time – no, one *meal* at a time – and before you know it, you'll find yourself saying: "I'm veggie, you know!"

You'll be vibrant and healthy, eating wonderful meals, doing your bit to help the world food supplies go round and make the world a healthier, fairer place, reducing global warming, saving the animals, improving your own health… what's not to love!

Be part of the growing movement: start today!

Rose Elliot MBE
Vegetarian Cookery Writer,
Patron of the Vegetarian Society

RoseElliot.com
@RoseElliotMBE

Introduction by the Vegetarian Society

This book comes to you by popular request!

We ran a New Year healthy eating campaign, Unstuffed, and thousands of people joined in. The campaign, which was run online, was all about delicious yet health-conscious meals put together into nutritionally balanced weekly meal plans. The recipes were specially created to appeal to meat-eaters wanting to reduce their meat intake, and also to vegetarians looking to follow a healthier diet. And it worked. Over half of the people taking part were meat-eaters and the rest were vegetarians wanting to eat more healthily.

The feedback we received was amazing – people told us how inspired and enthusiastic they were about the dishes we'd created. One question became a bit of a theme of the comments we received: "Are you putting all these recipes into a book?" Well, we love to please – so here it is!

The benefits of using these recipes in your diet are enormous. The dishes were all created with fibre and protein content in mind. Equally, wherever salt and added sugar are required (which is as little as possible), they've been used sparingly – or more often than not, replaced with a more health-focused ingredient. Of course, never at the expense of the taste.

This recipe collection is designed to be packed with wholegrains, nuts and seeds, which boost all sorts of nutrients in the diet, from protein and fibre, to minerals like zinc and selenium. Each recipe has a strong plant-focused basis, to which a moderate amount of eggs and low fat dairy are added to increase protein, vitamin and essential mineral intakes.

These dishes have been created with everyone in mind. If you are looking to increase the amount of plant-based meals you eat, this book is a great place to find nutritious meals packed with flavour. If you are already vegetarian, you'll find this book will provide a welcome dash of inspiration in the kitchen. In these pages you will find dishes that will fuel your body and excite your taste buds in equal measure.

Tasty, delicious, easy to prepare and already tested and enjoyed by thousands, we are really happy to bring these recipes to you. We hope you enjoy them as much as we do.

About the Vegetarian Society

The Vegetarian Society is a national charity that influences, inspires and supports people to embrace and maintain a vegetarian lifestyle. Being vegetarian is a choice that is kinder to animals, to people, and to our living planet. Established in 1847, we have been at the leading edge of the vegetarian community for over a century and a half.

Here's a taste of what we do...

The Vegetarian Society Cookery School runs courses for all tastes and abilities – from enthusiastic home cooks or those who quake at the thought of having to rustle up a meal, right through to professional chefs working in some of the finest restaurants. Our school also works with a variety of community groups and other organisations to offer free sessions and cookery demonstrations, reaching people who wouldn't ordinarily get to try vegetarian food.

We have an award-winning website with a wealth of information about vegetarian food including recipes, information on nutrition, reasons why people make the choice to eat more veggie food, the latest news and stories, and a whole host more. We also have very busy social media channels, which support hundreds of thousands of people interested in cooking, eating and enjoying veggie food.

When you've exhausted the recipes in this book, you can always take a look at our free recipe app for mobiles and tablets, which has over 750 more recipes to try.

And when you're out shopping, don't forget to look for our Vegetarian Society Approved trademark, carried by thousands of vegetarian products. The trademark gives you the assurance that what you're buying is truly vegetarian, which can make your weekly shop easier.

You can be part of this growing community and support our work. Join us for a healthy, tasty future.

www.vegsoc.org

Notes about the recipes in this book

All recipes in this book serve two people, unless otherwise stated.

The nutritional information given relates to typical values per serving, and is intended only as a guide.

Wherever eggs are used in the recipes, they are medium sized, unless otherwise stated.

When rinsing lentils, carefully check them for any stones before using.

The soya beans mentioned in these recipes are shelled soya beans, not soya beans still in their pods.

Now let's get cooking...

Kick-Start Your Day

Often referred to as 'the most important meal of the day', a good breakfast can really set you up for a busy morning.

In this section you'll find everything from light-but-delicious smoothies for when you are on-the-go, to heartier cooked breakfasts to keep hunger at bay until lunchtime.

Whether you're looking for something to begin a lazy Sunday or a crazy Monday, we've got it covered...

Bircher Muesli with Banana and Berries

Make this muesli the night before you want to eat it. You could replace some of the oats in this cereal with barley, spelt, quinoa or buckwheat flakes. With calcium-rich yogurt and fruits, this makes a nutrient-laden start to the day.

Ingredients

- ½ medium apple, grated
- 100g rolled oats
- 120ml cloudy apple juice
- 2 tsp lime juice
- 3 tbsp low fat natural yogurt
- 1 large banana
- 40g frozen berries, defrosted
- 2 tsp pumpkin seeds

Method

1. Combine the apple with the oats in a bowl.
2. Add apple juice and the lime juice. Then add the yogurt to the bowl and mix until all the oats are covered.
3. Cover the bowl and place in the fridge overnight.
4. Stir and add more yogurt if too thick. Serve with banana, berries and seeds.

Note: this keeps for two days in the fridge.

Preparation: 10 mins
(leave overnight)

Energy: 351 kcals Protein: 10.8g Carbohydrate: 60.2g Of which sugars: 27.7g Fat: 7.1g
Of which saturates: 2.5g Fibre: 7.7g Salt: 0.1g

Avocado, Seeds, Hazelnuts and Lentil Sprouts

Combining lentil sprouts with nuts means this dish contains all of the essential amino acids – making a complete protein. This dish works great as a nutritious topping for toast.

Ingredients

- 20g blanched hazelnuts, chopped
- 1 tbsp pumpkin seeds
- 2 medium avocados, halved and stone removed
- 50g lentil sprouts
- 1 tsp olive oil
- 10g fresh coriander, chopped
- 1 tbsp lemon juice
- 1 tbsp lime juice
- Pinch of salt
- Pinch of ground black pepper

Preparation: 5 mins
Cooking: 3 mins

Method

1. Warm a small frying pan over medium heat. Add the nuts and seeds and toast for a few minutes, stirring occasionally, until slightly browned. Do not leave the pan unattended, as nuts and seeds burn easily.

2. Transfer the nuts and seeds to a plate to cool.

3. Scoop out the avocado flesh and place in a large bowl along with the sprouts, cooled nuts and seeds.

4. Add the olive oil, coriander, citrus juices and season with salt and pepper.

5. Divide the mixture between two plates and serve.

Energy: 388 kcals Protein: 8.1g Carbohydrate: 10.6g Of which sugars: 1.5g Fat: 35.8g
Of which saturates: 6.4g Fibre: 7.1g Salt: 0.1g

Berry and Ginger Oat Breakfast Smoothie

This is a nutritious breakfast option providing a source of calcium and B vitamins. Perfect for people who want to eat on-the-go.

Ingredients

- ½ inch piece ginger, peeled and grated
- 40g rolled oats
- 250ml semi-skimmed milk
- 75g fresh or frozen berries
- 1 tbsp honey
- 2 tbsp low fat natural yogurt
- 3 ice cubes

Method

1. Put all the ingredients into a blender and blend until smooth.

2. Add a little water if the smoothie is too thick.

3. Pour into tall glasses and serve.

Preparation: 5 mins

Energy: 214 kcals Protein: 8.8g Carbohydrate: 35.5g Of which sugars: 22.1g Fat: 4.1g
Of which saturates: 2.3g Fibre: 2.8g Salt: 0.2g

Banana, Raspberry, Coconut and Oat Smoothie

Bananas are rich in potassium and a good source of vitamin B6 which helps to convert food into energy.

Ingredients

- Handful of ice
- 80g frozen raspberries
- 125g low fat natural yogurt
- 1 large banana
- 45g rolled oats
- 125ml coconut water
- 1 tsp honey

Method

1. Simply blend all the ingredients together in a blender and serve.

Preparation: 5 mins

Energy: **212 kcals** Protein: **7g** Carbohydrate: **40.5g** Of which sugars: **25.4g** Fat: **2.4g**
Of which saturates: **1.3g** Fibre: **4.5g** Salt: **0.1g**

Scrambled Tofu with Spinach and Tomatoes

Tofu not only provides a good source of meat-free protein but is also a useful source of calcium, which is essential to maintaining good bone health.

Ingredients

- 400g firm tofu, drained and mashed
- ½ tsp turmeric
- Pinch of salt
- Pinch of ground black pepper
- 1 tsp olive oil
- 1 medium red onion or 3 spring onions, finely diced
- 100g spinach, stems removed and roughly chopped
- 1 tbsp lemon juice
- 100g cherry tomatoes, chopped
- 2 medium slices wholemeal or granary sliced bread, toasted
- 2 level tsp low fat spread

Preparation: 10 mins
Cooking: 10 mins

Method

1. Into a bowl, place the tofu, turmeric, salt and pepper and combine well.

2. Heat the oil in a large, non-stick frying pan over a medium heat.

3. Add the onion and cook for 2 minutes until softened.

4. Add in the tofu mixture and continue to cook, stirring occasionally until the tofu is lightly browned and resembles scrambled egg.

5. Add in the spinach with the lemon juice, stirring until the spinach wilts, then add the cherry tomatoes and stir until the tomatoes begin to soften.

6. Serve with the toasted slices of wholemeal or granary bread and low fat spread.

Energy: 315 kcals Protein: 23.3g Carbohydrate: 26.6g Of which sugars: 8.3g Fat: 13.3g
Of which saturates: 1.9g Fibre: 6.2g Salt: 0.7g

Blueberry Pancakes with Maple Syrup and Hazelnuts

Combining wholemeal flour with white is a good way to increase your intake of fibre, a nutrient that is lacking in the average UK diet.

Ingredients

- 25g wholemeal plain flour
- 25g plain flour
- 1 tsp baking powder
- ½ tsp ground cinnamon
- 1 free-range egg
- 75ml semi-skimmed milk
- 140g fresh or frozen blueberries
- 20g blanched hazelnuts
- 2 tsp olive oil
- 2 tsp maple syrup

Preparation: 10 mins
Cooking: 10 mins

Method

1. Combine the dry ingredients in a mixing bowl and make a well in the centre. Pour the egg and half of the milk into the well, then beat this mixture into a thick batter. Stir through the remaining milk.

2. Add the berries and stir.

3. Heat a large non-stick frying pan over a low heat and add the hazelnuts. Toast gently for a few minutes then transfer to a plate and set aside to cool before chopping. Wipe the pan clean then brush the base with olive oil.

4. Add the mixture a single tablespoon at a time (to make each pancake).

5. As soon as bubbles start to rise to the surface of the pancakes, flip them over using a palette knife and cook the other side for about 30 seconds. The pancakes should be golden brown in colour.

6. Lift the pancakes out of the pan and place on a warm plate.

7. Repeat steps 4 to 6 until all of the batter has been used.

8. Serve with the maple syrup and the chopped toasted hazelnuts.

Potato Pancakes with Eggs and Tomatoes

Eggs are a nutritional powerhouse and are particularly rich in B vitamins which help to maintain healthy skin.

Ingredients

For the potato pancakes:
- 1 medium potato, peeled and cut into even-sized pieces
- 35g wholemeal plain flour
- ½ tsp baking powder
- 1 free-range egg
- 125ml semi-skimmed milk
- A few chives, finely chopped
- 1 tsp olive oil

For the eggs and tomatoes:
- 2 tsp olive oil
- 1 clove garlic, sliced
- 2 medium tomatoes, halved
- 4 medium free-range eggs, beaten

Method

1. Bring a small saucepan of water to the boil, add the potato and cook for 15 to 20 minutes until just soft. Drain, then place back in the pan and mash. Leave to cool slightly.

2. Sieve the flour and baking powder onto the cooled mashed potatoes. Whisk the egg and milk together and add to the potato mix with the chives. Mix well until smooth.

3. Heat a large non-stick frying pan over a medium heat, add ½ tsp olive oil and then add three single tablespoons of potato pancake mixture in different areas of the pan. Cook for about 1 minute until the underside is golden brown and small bubbles appear. Flip the pancakes over and cook the other side until golden.

4. Remove from the pan and keep warm while cooking the remaining pancakes in the same way, adding the remaining oil to the pan. Keep the pancakes warm.

5. Heat 1 tsp oil in a small frying pan and add the sliced garlic. Cook gently until golden in colour then add the tomatoes. Cook gently for 2 minutes then remove from the pan and keep warm with the pancakes.

6. Add the remaining 1 tsp olive oil to the same pan the tomatoes were in and add the beaten eggs, then stir until cooked.

7. Serve the pancakes with tomatoes and eggs.

Preparation: 10 mins
Cooking: 30 mins

Energy: **416 kcals** Protein: **24g** Carbohydrate: **30.6g** Of which sugars: **6.5g** Fat: **22.8g**
Of which saturates: **6g** Fibre: **4.7g** Salt: **0.9g**

Huevos Rancheros (Eggs, Tomatoes and Peppers)

This dish is bursting with nutrients, from the mineral-rich eggs to the peppers and tomatoes that are rich in antioxidants such as vitamin C and the nutrient lycopene.

Ingredients

- 1 tbsp olive oil
- 1 clove garlic, finely chopped
- 1 small onion, finely chopped
- 1 large red pepper, seeds removed and discarded, finely chopped
- 1 small red chilli, finely chopped
- 1 tsp tomato purée
- ½ tsp ground cumin
- 1 x 400g can chopped tomatoes
- 4 medium free-range eggs
- 2 large wholemeal wraps
- 2 tbsp sour cream

Preparation: 10 mins
Cooking: 35 mins

Method

1. Preheat the oven to 180°C / gas mark 4.

2. In a pan large enough for four eggs, heat the oil. Add the garlic, onion, red pepper and red chilli and cook on a low heat for 5 minutes. When soft, but not browning, turn the heat up. Add the tomato purée and cumin and let the mixture bubble for 1 minute. Add the can of chopped tomatoes. Cook for 20 minutes over a medium heat. If it begins to dry out, add a little water.

3. When the sauce is reduced make four holes and crack the eggs into them. Let the eggs fry, occasionally basting with the tomato sauce.

4. While the eggs are cooking place the wraps in the oven and bake for 2 minutes until warm then remove and place them on separate plates.

5. When the eggs are cooked, spoon two on top of each of the tortillas and share the sauce between them.

6. Serve with a dollop of sour cream.

Salads and Light Bites

Lighter meals can often hit the spot – just enough to fill you up without slowing you down.

Salad dishes are perfect for a quick, light meal – and by combining different colours, textures and flavours, they need never be boring.

By including a variety of food groups in a single dish, the light option can often be the right option...

Wild Rice, Broad Bean and Walnut Salad

Walnuts are a rich source of the plant-based omega-3 fatty acid called alpha-linolenic acid.

Ingredients

- 80g wild rice (or red or brown rice)
- 50g broad beans, frozen
- 1 clove garlic, crushed
- 2 large spring onions, sliced
- 4 medium radishes, sliced
- 2 small sticks celery, chopped
- 50g spinach, chopped
- 1 small avocado, peeled, stoned and cubed
- 20g walnuts, chopped
- 2 tsp olive oil
- 1 tsp lemon juice
- Pinch of salt
- Pinch of ground black pepper
- Lemon wedge (to serve)

Method

1. Bring a pan of water to the boil and add the wild rice. Cook for approximately 40 minutes until the grains have 'popped'. (If using red or brown rice, adjust the cooking times according to packet instructions.)

2. While the rice is cooking, prepare the vegetables and walnuts.

3. Warm a small non-stick frying pan over medium heat and gently toast the walnuts for a few minutes, stirring occasionally. Keep a close eye on the pan as walnuts burn easily.

4. When the rice has 5 minutes left to cook, add the frozen broad beans to the rice.

5. Once cooked, drain the rice and broad beans in a colander or sieve and run under cold water to cool.

6. Add the rice, beans, vegetables and walnuts to a large mixing bowl and stir in the olive oil and lemon juice until well mixed.

7. Season with salt and pepper then serve garnished with a wedge of lemon.

Preparation: 20 mins
Cooking: 45 mins

Energy: **363 kcals** Protein: **11.1g** Carbohydrate: **33.7g** Of which sugars: **3.4g** Fat: **20.6g** Of which saturates: **3.4g** Fibre: **8.4g** Salt: **0.1g**

Roasted Cauliflower, Grape and Wensleydale Salad

Cauliflower is a very rich source of vitamin C, which plays a key role in maintaining a healthy immune system. A single serving of this dish provides half of your recommended daily intake.

Ingredients

- 1 medium cauliflower, broken into small florets
- 2 tbsp olive oil
- Pinch of salt
- Pinch of ground black pepper
- 1 tbsp red wine vinegar
- 1 tsp Dijon mustard
- 25g sultanas
- 40g vegetarian Wensleydale cheese, crumbled
- 60g seedless red grapes
- 2 tbsp walnuts, crushed
- 1 tbsp mixed seeds
- 10g fresh parsley, chopped

Method

1. Preheat the oven to 200°C / gas mark 6.

2. Put the cauliflower into a bowl and toss with 1 tbsp of the oil and season with salt and pepper. Spread on an oven tray and roast for 20 to 25 minutes, turning once or twice, until nicely browned. Set aside to cool.

3. Meanwhile, in a bowl mix the remaining oil with the vinegar and mustard. Add the sultanas and leave to soak while the cauliflower is cooking.

4. Transfer the cauliflower to a bowl with the cheese and grapes and toss together with the sultana dressing. Sprinkle with walnuts, seeds and parsley then serve.

Preparation: 15 mins
Cooking: 25 mins

Energy: **414 kcals** Protein: **13.1g** Carbohydrate: **18.4g** Of which sugars: **16.7g** Fat: **32.3g**
Of which saturates: **7.4g** Fibre: **4.6g** Salt: **0.6g**   29

Black Bean and Avocado Salad

This dish provides one-third of your recommended daily intake of magnesium. This mineral is involved in many reactions in the body and is essential for healthy bones and the conversion of food into energy.

Ingredients

- 100g green beans, topped and tailed and cut into 1cm pieces
- 2 tbsp pumpkin seeds
- 1 x 400g can black beans, drained and washed
- 1 small onion, finely diced
- 2 tsp olive oil
- 1 tbsp lime juice
- ½ tsp ground cumin
- 2 large spring onion, finely sliced
- 1 stick celery, finely sliced
- 10g fresh coriander
- Pinch of salt
- Pinch of ground black pepper
- 1 large avocado, peeled, stoned and sliced

Preparation: 8 mins
Cooking: 3 mins

Method

1. Bring a small saucepan of water to the boil and blanch the green beans for 1 minute. Drain the beans and run under cold water so they retain their colour.

2. Heat a small frying pan and add the pumpkin seeds. Move the seeds around the pan to evenly toast them for a couple of minutes then remove from the heat and set aside to cool.

3. Place the black beans in a medium mixing bowl with the green beans and all remaining ingredients, except the avocado, and combine well and season.

4. Serve the bean mixture in small bowls and top with the slices of avocado.

Quinoa, Avocado and Spinach Salad

Quinoa is a brilliant grain to include in a vegetarian diet as it contains all of the essential amino acids that are needed by the body.

Ingredients

- 40g cashew nuts
- 120g quinoa
- 1 medium red onion, finely sliced
- 2 sticks celery, finely sliced
- 1 medium avocado, peeled, stoned and cut into chunks
- 80g spinach, roughly chopped
- 1 small yellow pepper, seeds removed and discarded, finely chopped
- 15g fresh coriander, finely chopped
- Pinch of salt
- Pinch of ground black pepper
- 1 tbsp olive oil
- 2 tbsp lemon juice

Method

1. Warm a small frying pan over a medium heat and add the cashew nuts. Gently toast the nuts for 2 to 3 minutes until lightly browned. Transfer the cashews to a small plate to cool.

2. Rinse the quinoa then add it to a saucepan of cold water and bring to the boil. Cook for a further 5 minutes or until the seeds start to 'burst' and are tender.

3. Drain the quinoa, then transfer to a large bowl along with the vegetables, coriander and cashew nuts. Mix well.

4. Season the salad with salt and pepper, dress with olive oil and lemon juice, then serve.

Preparation: 15 mins
Cooking: 10 mins

Energy: **545 kcals** Protein: **16.2g** Carbohydrate: **48.0g** Of which sugars: **12.7g** Fat: **33.5g** Of which saturates: **6.1g** Fibre: **8.3g** Salt: **0.4g**

Beetroot, Puy Lentils and Spinach Salad

Beetroot is thought to increase bile production which helps the liver with the natural detoxification process.

Ingredients

For the salad:
- 100g Puy lentils, rinsed
- 100g spinach, washed, roughly chopped
- 150g cooked beetroot (not in vinegar), cut into small cubes
- 2 tbsp walnuts, chopped
- Pinch of salt
- Pinch of ground black pepper

For the dressing:
- 1 tbsp wholegrain mustard
- 1 tbsp walnut oil
- Pinch of salt
- Pinch of ground black pepper

To serve:
- 2 medium slices wholemeal or granary bread

Method

1. Place the lentils in a pan of cold water, bring to the boil, then simmer for 15 minutes until the lentils are tender, but with a bite. Drain the lentils and leave them to cool.

2. While the lentils are cooling, make the dressing by mixing the mustard and oil together with salt and pepper.

3. Put the lentils into a bowl with the chopped spinach, pour over the dressing and mix well. Stir through the beetroot and season to taste.

4. Divide the salad into bowls, sprinkle with walnuts and serve with bread.

Preparation: 10 mins
Cooking: 15 mins

Energy: **449 kcals** Protein: **21.7g** Carbohydrate: **49.8g** Of which sugars: **10.0g** Fat: **18.6g** Of which saturates: **2.0g** Fibre: **13.6g** Salt: **1.3g**

Roasted Beetroot, Feta Cheese and Apple Salad

Beetroot is a very rich source of potassium which is essential for maintaining fluid balance in the body and is associated with healthy blood pressure.

Ingredients

For the salad:
- 3 medium beetroots, topped and tailed, peeled and cut into bite-size chunks
- 25g walnut halves
- 100g quinoa

- ½ small red onion, finely sliced
- 1 medium apple, peeled, cored and finely sliced
- 50g spinach
- 60g vegetarian feta cheese

For the dressing:
- 2 tbsp lemon juice
- 1 tbsp olive oil
- Fresh flat leaf parsley, finely chopped
- Pinch of ground black pepper
- Pinch of salt

Method

1. Preheat the oven to 180°C / gas mark 4.

2. Wrap the beetroot chunks loosely in tin foil and place in the oven on a baking sheet for about 20 to 25 minutes until they are tender but still have a crunch. While the beetroot is cooking, scatter the walnuts over the baking sheet and cook for 2 minutes, then carefully remove from the baking sheet and set aside. Once the beetroot is cooked, remove from the oven, drain any excess liquid and leave to cool.

3. Place the quinoa in a saucepan of cold water and bring to the boil. Cook for a further 5 minutes or until the seeds start to 'burst' and are tender. Drain with a sieve and set aside to cool.

4. Make the salad dressing by putting the lemon juice, olive oil, parsley and seasoning in a small bowl and whisking together.

5. Construct the salad by dividing the quinoa between two salad bowls and placing the remaining ingredients on top. Finally, sprinkle with crumbled feta cheese and drizzle with dressing.

Energy: **452 kcals** Protein: **16.9g** Carbohydrate: **46.8g** Of which sugars: **20.8g** Fat: **23.2g**
Of which saturates: **6.2g** Fibre: **6g** Salt: **1.5g**

Greek Salad with Avocado

This colourful salad provides a good source of calcium and healthy fats.

Ingredients

- 100g cucumber, seeds removed and chopped into small chunks
- 2 medium tomatoes, chopped
- 50g spinach, sliced
- 1 small red onion, sliced
- 10g fresh flat leaf parsley, finely chopped
- 1 medium avocado, peeled, halved, stoned and cut into cubes
- 6 black olives, pitted and halved
- 1 tbsp lemon juice
- 1 tbsp olive oil
- Pinch of salt
- Pinch of ground black pepper
- 120g vegetarian feta cheese, cubed

Method

1. Place the first seven ingredients in a large bowl and combine with the lemon juice and olive oil.

2. Season the salad with salt and pepper then divide the salad between two plates and sprinkle each with feta cheese.

Preparation: 10 mins

Energy: 358 kcals Protein: 12g Carbohydrate: 10.1g Of which sugars: 7.7g Fat: 30g
Of which saturates: 10.7g Fibre: 7.2g Salt: 2.5g

Aubergine, Chickpea, Pomegranate and Feta Cheese Salad

Aubergines are low in calories and high in fibre.

Ingredients

- 2 large aubergines, cut lengthways into thick slices
- 1 tbsp olive oil
- 1 tbsp red wine vinegar
- 1 x 210g can chickpeas, drained and rinsed
- Pinch of salt
- Pinch of ground black pepper
- 80g pomegranate seeds
- 15g fresh flat leaf parsley, chopped
- 10g fresh mint, chopped
- 100g vegetarian feta cheese

Preparation: 15 mins
Cooking: 20 mins

Method

1. Heat a griddle pan or large non-stick frying pan over a high heat.

2. Place the slices of aubergine on the pan and cook each side for 3 minutes until lightly charred and tender. Once each slice is cooked, place them all in a large bowl and cover with cling film. Leave for 15 minutes.

3. Make the dressing by combining the oil and vinegar in a small bowl and whisking.

4. Transfer the chickpeas to a large bowl.

5. Take each aubergine slice and roughly tear into strips (you can also use kitchen scissors for this) then add to the bowl with the chickpeas.

6. Add the dressing to the bowl and combine, adding in salt and pepper. Next, throw in the pomegranate seeds, parsley and mint leaves then lightly toss.

7. Divide the aubergine mixture between 2 plates and sprinkle with feta cheese before serving.

Avocado and Lentil Salad

Avocados are a source of monounsaturated fats and folic acid. Both of these nutrients are associated with good heart health, making this dish the perfect healthy lunch.

Ingredients

- 60g Puy lentils, rinsed
- 250ml low sodium vegetable stock
- 1 tbsp olive oil
- 2 tbsp wholegrain mustard
- 1 tbsp white wine vinegar
- Pinch of salt
- Pinch of ground black pepper
- 150g Savoy cabbage, washed and shredded
- 1 medium avocado, peeled, stoned and cut into small chunks
- 2 tbsp lemon juice

To serve:
- 2 large wholemeal pitta bread

Method

1. Place the lentils in a saucepan, then add vegetable stock and simmer for 15 to 20 minutes until tender but still with a bite.

2. While the lentils are cooking, make the dressing by mixing together the olive oil, mustard, vinegar, salt and pepper.

3. Drain the lentils and return them to the pan. Add half of the dressing while the lentils are still warm and combine well. Set aside to cool.

4. Blanch the prepared cabbage in boiling water for 1 minute, then drain and rinse under cold water. Drain again.

5. In a large bowl add the lentils, cabbage and avocado. Add the lemon juice and the remaining dressing and combine well.

6. Serve with warmed wholemeal pitta bread.

Energy: **423 kcals** Protein: **18.2g** Carbohydrate: **40.5g** Of which sugars: **6.4g** Fat: **17.3g** Of which saturates: **3.4g** Fibre: **20.2g** Salt: **1.9g**

Nutty Tabbouleh Salad

The addition of nuts and seeds to this tabbouleh recipe adds protein, healthy fats, B vitamins, magnesium and iron making it a substantial lunch option.

Ingredients

- 120g couscous
- 180ml low sodium vegetable stock, hot
- 1 tbsp unsalted pistachio nuts, shelled
- 1 tbsp pine nuts
- 1 tbsp sunflower seeds
- 1 small red pepper, seeds removed and discarded, chopped
- 1 large courgette, chopped
- 2 large spring onions, finely chopped
- 10g fresh mint, finely chopped
- 15g fresh flat leaf parsley, finely chopped
- 4 dried apricots, sliced into thin strips
- 6 cherry tomatoes, halved
- 1 tbsp olive oil
- ½ tsp ground cumin
- 2 tbsp lemon juice
- Pinch of salt
- Pinch of ground black pepper

Method

1. Place the couscous in a small shallow bowl or saucepan. Pour over the hot stock, stir and then cover. Leave to sit for 5 minutes then separate with a fork.

2. Heat a small saucepan over a medium heat. Add the pistachio nuts and pine nuts and toast for 2 minutes until they start to colour. Don't leave the pan and keep the nuts moving as they can burn easily. Once toasted, transfer to a plate and leave to cool.

3. Place the cooked couscous in a mixing bowl, add all of the other ingredients and combine well before serving.

Preparation: 10 mins
Cooking: 5 mins

Energy: **496 kcals** Protein: **15.6g** Carbohydrate: **65.3g** Of which sugars: **16g** Fat: **19.6g**
Of which saturates: **2.4g** Fibre: **9.7g** Salt: **0.6g**

Paneer, Roasted Beetroot and Hazelnut Salad

Hazelnuts contain monounsaturated fats which are a healthier type of fat that benefit the heart.

Ingredients

For the salad:
- 300g beetroot, peeled and cut into wedges
- 1 tbsp olive oil
- 30g blanched hazelnuts
- 75g vegetarian paneer, cut into 2-3cm cubes
- 50g watercress

For the dressing:
- 1 heaped tbsp low fat natural yogurt
- 1 tbsp lemon juice
- ½ tsp horseradish sauce
- 1 tsp dried dill

To serve:
- 2 large wholemeal pitta breads

Preparation: 5 mins
Cooking: 40 mins

Method

1. Preheat the oven to 180°C / gas mark 4.
2. Put the beetroot wedges in a roasting tin, drizzle with 1 tsp olive oil and roast for 30 minutes.
3. Add the hazelnuts to the roasting tin and roast for a further 5 minutes.
4. While the beetroot is roasting, heat the remaining 2 tsp oil in a frying pan and add the paneer, cooking over a low heat until brown on all sides.
5. Make the dressing by mixing together the yogurt, lemon juice, horseradish and dill.
6. Mix the beetroot wedges and hazelnuts, paneer, dressing and watercress together in a large bowl.
7. Serve with pitta bread.

Midday Meals

By the time lunchtime comes around, we need to refuel. But with busy lifestyles, it's all too easy to slip into the habit of always having the same old sandwich or soup.

If you're looking for a tasty lunch that can bring inspiration to your afternoon, flick through the next few pages.

Go on – make your midday meal a legend in your own lunchtime...

Winter Roots and Beans Soup

This homemade soup is packed with nutrients, offering three servings of vegetables, plenty of fibre, and more than a third of your daily intake for most vitamins and minerals per bowl.

Ingredients

- 2 tsp olive oil
- 2 cloves garlic, crushed
- 1 small onion, finely diced
- 1 medium swede, peeled and chopped into chunks
- 3 large carrots, peeled and chopped into chunks
- 1 medium parsnip, peeled and chopped into chunks
- 4 sprigs thyme, stalks removed
- 850ml low sodium vegetable stock
- 550ml semi-skimmed milk
- 2 x 400g can mixed beans
- Pinch of ground black pepper
- 1 medium wholemeal or granary French baguette

Serves: 4
Preparation: 10 mins
Cooking: 40 mins

Method

1. Heat the oil in a large saucepan then add the garlic and onion, frying over a medium heat for 5 minutes or until soft but not coloured.

2. Add the prepared swede, carrot, parsnip and sprigs of thyme, then stir to combine.

3. Add the stock and milk, bring to the boil then simmer for 15 to 20 minutes until the vegetables are tender.

4. While the vegetables are cooking, drain the canned mixed beans into a colander and rinse.

5. When the vegetables are tender, remove from the heat and put one-third into a food processor or blender, then blend until smooth.

6. Return the blended mixture to the pan, add the beans, stir and warm through over a low heat.

7. Season the soup with black pepper to taste.

8. Serve the soup in bowls with half of the French baguette per person.

Cannellini Bean, Potato and Tomato Soup

Tomatoes are a rich source of lycopene, which may be associated with reducing the risk of prostate cancer.

Ingredients

- 1 tbsp olive oil
- ½ tsp fennel seeds
- 1 small red onion, roughly chopped
- 1 medium carrot, peeled and roughly chopped
- 1 stick celery, roughly chopped
- 2 cloves garlic, crushed
- ½ x 400g can chopped tomatoes
- 1 medium tomato, chopped
- 1 bay leaf
- ½ x 400g cannellini beans, drained
- 1 small potato, peeled and cubed
- 150g kale, finely sliced
- 50g stale bread, torn into chunks
- Pinch of salt
- Pinch of ground black pepper
- 2 tsp vegetarian pesto

Method

1. Pour the olive oil into a medium-sized saucepan and heat the fennel seeds until they pop. Add the onion, carrot, celery and garlic and cook over a low heat with the lid ajar for 15 minutes until soft, but not brown.

2. Add the canned and fresh tomatoes and bay leaf then bring back to a gentle simmer for a few minutes.

3. Add the cannellini beans and potato, together with 100ml water, and bring back to the boil and simmer for 15 minutes.

4. Stir in the kale and the bread and continue cooking for a further 15 minutes. The soup should be thick but not dry, so add more water if needed.

5. Serve in bowls, seasoned to taste, topped with a dollop of pesto.

Preparation: 15 mins
Cooking: 45 mins

Energy: **358 kcals** Protein: **15.7g** Carbohydrate: **45.6g** Of which sugars: **11.7g** Fat: **12.5g**
Of which saturates: **1.1g** Fibre: **11.7g** Salt: **0.8g**

Butter Bean, Spinach and Sun-Dried Tomato Wrap

Sun-dried tomatoes are rich in lycopene which is an antioxidant often associated with men's health.

Ingredients

- 1 x 210g can butter beans, drained with liquid reserved
- 1 clove garlic, crushed
- 1 tsp olive oil
- 1 tsp lemon juice
- Pinch of ground black pepper
- 2 large tortilla wraps
- A few drops of Tabasco
- 100g spinach leaves
- 6 sun-dried tomatoes, sliced

Method

1. In a food processor, blend the butter beans with a little of their reserved liquid to make a thick, creamy purée.

2. Stir the garlic through the puréed beans with the lemon juice, olive oil and black pepper.

3. Spread the bean mixture over the wraps then add a few drops of Tabasco sauce to taste.

4. Add the spinach and sun-dried tomatoes then roll, slicing each wrap in half diagonally before serving.

Preparation: 10 mins

Energy: **385 kcals** Protein: **15.2g** Carbohydrate: **68.6g** Of which sugars: **3.3g** Fat: **7.5g**
Of which saturates: **1.1g** Fibre: **12.3g** Salt: **2.1g**

Halloumi, Red Pepper, Spinach and Harissa Wrap

Wraps make for a versatile lunch option and can be filled with any number of nutritious food combinations. This wrap provides over half of the recommended daily intake of calcium.

Ingredients

For the filling:
- 1 large red pepper, seeds removed and discarded, cut into strips
- 1 tsp olive oil
- 100g vegetarian halloumi, sliced
- 50g spinach, chopped

For the dressing:
- 1 heaped tbsp low fat natural yogurt
- 3 leaves fresh mint, chopped
- 1 tsp harissa paste

For the wrap:
- 2 large wholemeal tortilla wraps

Method

1. Preheat the oven to 180°C / gas mark 4.

2. Place the pepper strips on a baking sheet, brush with the olive oil, then bake for about 10 to 15 minutes until softened. Remove from the oven and set aside to cool.

3. Heat a small frying pan or griddle and add the halloumi slices, cooking for 2 minutes on either side.

4. Make the dressing by combining the yogurt, mint and harissa paste.

5. To build the wraps, spread each tortilla with dressing, add a layer of spinach, then top with the halloumi slices and red pepper. Fold the wrap as preferred and serve.

Energy: **331 kcals** Protein: **16g** Carbohydrate: **44.5g** Of which sugars: **8.9g** Fat: **10.7g**
Of which saturates: **5g** Fibre: **4.6g** Salt: **3.5g**

Carrot, Beetroot and Harissa Hummus Flatbread

This dish is a rich source of folate, which may benefit heart health in people with high levels of homocysteine in the blood (a risk factor for heart disease).

Ingredients

- 25g pine nuts
- 100g hummus
- 1 tsp harissa
- 1 large carrot, peeled and grated
- 2 medium beetroots, peeled and grated
- 2 tsp lemon juice
- 2 large wholemeal flatbreads
- ½ small red onion, finely sliced
- 50g spinach, finely sliced
- 10g fresh flat leaf parsley, finely chopped
- Pinch of salt

Method

1. Set a small frying pan over a medium heat and add the pine nuts. Toast until golden brown taking care not to burn them.

2. Combine the hummus with the harissa in a bowl.

3. In another bowl add the carrot, beetroot and lemon juice and combine well.

4. Lay each flatbread out and spread with the hummus and harissa mixture. Now place the red onion, spinach and parsley on top of the hummus. Finally spoon over the carrot and beetroot and sprinkle with the toasted pine nuts.

5. Season with a pinch of salt and roll each wrap, then cut in half to serve.

Preparation: 10 mins
Cooking: 1 min

Energy: **317 kcals** Protein: **11.8g** Carbohydrate: **46.7g** Of which sugars: **12.7g** Fat: **9.3g** Of which saturates: **1.2g** Fibre: **10.1g** Salt: **1.9g**

Lentil and Avocado Lettuce Wraps

Using lettuce in place of flour tortillas is a great way to reduce calorie content.

Ingredients

For the wraps:
• 1 head iceberg or butter lettuce, washed and large leaves removed and kept

For the filling:
• 1 tbsp extra virgin coconut oil
• ½ small onion, finely chopped
• 180g lentil sprout mix
• 2 large carrots, peeled and grated
• 1 large avocado, peeled, stoned and sliced
• 1 large mango, peeled, stoned and cut into thin strips

For the dressing:
• 100g low fat natural yogurt
• 15g tahini
• 2 tsp lime juice
• ½ clove garlic, crushed
• ½ inch piece ginger, peeled and grated
• 1 tbsp olive oil
• ½ tsp turmeric

Preparation: 10 mins
Cooking: 5 mins

Method

1. Heat the coconut oil in a small pan over a medium heat and add the onion. Gently cook the onion for about 5 minutes until it is soft, then turn off the heat.

2. Add the lentil sprouts to the pan and combine with the onion.

3. Make the dressing by placing all the dressing ingredients in a bowl with 2 tsp of water and whisking together.

4. Start to build the wraps by laying out the lettuce leaves. First add the lentil sprouts followed by the carrot, avocado and mango, then top each wrap with a little dressing.

Tomato Bruschetta with Rocket and Butter Bean Salad

Beans and pulses are a really useful way to increase your intake of minerals such as zinc and iron, both of which have a role to play in maintaining a strong and healthy immune system.

Ingredients

For the bruschetta:
- 3 medium tomatoes, diced
- ½ small red onion, finely diced
- 1 clove garlic, finely chopped
- 5g fresh basil leaves, torn
- Pinch of salt
- Pinch of ground black pepper
- 4 medium slices ciabatta

For the salad:
- 1 x 210g can butter beans, drained and rinsed
- 10g fresh flat leaf parsley, chopped
- 1 small yellow pepper, seeds removed and discarded, finely diced
- 100g rocket
- 1 tbsp lemon juice
- 1 tbsp olive oil

Method

1. Preheat the grill to a medium heat.
2. In a bowl, combine the tomatoes, onion, garlic and basil. Season with salt and pepper. Set aside.
3. In another bowl, add the butter beans, parsley, yellow pepper, rocket, lemon juice and 1 tsp of the olive oil. Season.
4. Toast the ciabatta slices until golden brown, about 2 to 4 minutes per side. Once toasted, brush each slice with the remaining olive oil.
5. Spoon the tomato mixture on top of the bread slices and serve with the butter bean salad.

Preparation: 10 mins
Cooking: 4 mins

Energy: **358 kcals** Protein: **16.5g** Carbohydrate: **56g** Of which sugars: **12.6g** Fat: **8.5g** Of which saturates: **1.5g** Fibre: **14.7g** Salt: **0.9g**

Baked Mushrooms with Ciabatta

Mushrooms are a good source of vitamin B2, also known as riboflavin. This vitamin is essential for the body to be able to use energy from food and will help keep you going throughout the day.

Ingredients

- 2 large portobello mushrooms
- 1 large spring onion, finely sliced
- ½ clove garlic, finely sliced
- 1 sprig fresh thyme, leaves removed
- 60g vegetarian Brie, sliced
- 25g fresh or store-bought breadcrumbs
- 1 tsp fresh flat leaf parsley, finely chopped
- ½ loaf ciabatta bread

Preparation: 5 mins
Cooking: 20 mins

Method

1. Preheat the oven to 200°C / gas mark 6.

2. Lay the mushrooms on a baking tray and sprinkle with the spring onion, garlic and leaves from the thyme. Place Brie slices on top of each mushroom and cover with a mixture of breadcrumbs and parsley.

3. Bake in the oven for 15 to 20 minutes until the breadcrumbs are brown and the mushrooms are cooked through.

4. Meanwhile slice the ciabatta into two pieces and lightly toast.

5. Place a mushroom on top of each slice of toast and serve.

Energy: **327 kcals** Protein: **15.8g** Carbohydrate: **41.8g** Of which sugars: **2.6g** Fat: **11.9g**
Of which saturates: **5.9g** Fibre: **4.2g** Salt: **1.5g** 53

Broad Beans on Toast with Egg and Watercress

Eggs make a very healthy quick meal and are a good source of minerals such as zinc, selenium and iron, which help to support a strong immune system.

Ingredients

- 100g broad beans, frozen
- 2 tbsp olive oil
- ½ clove garlic
- Pinch of ground nutmeg
- Pinch of ground black pepper
- 2 free-range eggs
- 2 thick slices sourdough bread
- 100g watercress
- 1 tbsp lemon juice
- Pinch of salt
- A few chives, chopped

Preparation: 10 mins
Cooking: 10 mins

Method

1. Set a small saucepan of water over a medium heat and bring to the boil. Add the beans and cook for 4 to 6 minutes until tender. Drain and put into a blender with 1 tbsp olive oil, garlic, nutmeg and black pepper. Blend lightly to a coarse texture.
2. Heat 1 tbsp olive oil in a small, non-stick frying pan, crack in the eggs and fry.
3. While the eggs are frying, toast or grill the bread and then place on a plate and drizzle with a little oil.
4. Place watercress on each plate alongside the toasted sourdough and coat with the lemon juice, a dash of oil and a pinch of salt.
5. Spoon the beans over the toast and sit a fried egg on top, then sprinkle with chives.

Energy: **345 kcals** Protein: **16.1g** Carbohydrate: **28.6g** Of which sugars: **2.7g** Fat: **19.3g**
Of which saturates: **3.8g** Fibre: **6.7g** Salt: **1.1g**

Leek, Kale and Herb Omelette with Green Salad

Preparation: 10 mins
Cooking: 20 mins

Leeks are a good source of prebiotics that help good bacteria in the gut to flourish.

Ingredients

For the salad:
- 80g salad leaves
- 1 tsp lemon juice
- 1 tsp olive oil

For the omelette:
- 6 free-range eggs
- 5g flat leaf parsley, finely chopped
- 3g chives, finely chopped
- Pinch of salt
- Pinch of ground black pepper
- 2 tsp olive oil
- 100g leeks, thoroughly washed and thinly sliced
- 50g kale, stalks removed and discarded, finely sliced

Method

1. Toss the salad leaves with the lemon juice and olive oil then set aside.

2. Whisk together the eggs, herbs, salt and pepper.

3. Heat the oil in a non-stick omelette pan and sweat the leeks and kale for 2 minutes, stirring frequently, until they are slightly softened.

4. Add the egg and herb mixture to the pan.

5. When the egg starts to set on the outside and pull away from the side of the pan, flip it over to cook the other side for a few minutes.

6. Fold the omelette in half and remove from the pan.

7. Cut the omelette in two and serve each half on a plate with the salad leaves.

Energy: **329 kcals** Protein: **22.9g** Carbohydrate: **3.2g** Of which sugars: **2.9g** Fat: **25g**
Of which saturates: **6.2g** Fibre: **3.2g** Salt: **0.7g**

Portobello Mushrooms with Halloumi

Mushrooms have the ability to convert sunlight into vitamin D. It is common for people in the UK to have low levels of vitamin D.

Ingredients

- 300g portobello mushrooms
- 1 tbsp olive oil
- Pinch of ground black pepper
- 60g vegetarian halloumi
- 120g store-bought rocket and watercress salad
- 1 tbsp store-bought salad dressing
- 200g wholemeal or granary baguette

Preparation: 5 mins
Cooking: 10 mins

Method

1. Preheat the grill to medium/high.

2. Place the mushrooms on a grill tray, skin side down, brush with oil, season with pepper and grill for 5 minutes.

3. Put a slice of halloumi on top of each mushroom and grill for another 5 minutes until the cheese has browned and crisped on top.

4. Arrange the mushrooms on the plate with the rocket salad and spoon a little salad dressing over each.

5. Serve with slices of wholemeal baguette.

Energy: **395 kcals** Protein: **21.8g** Carbohydrate: **46g** Of which sugars: **5.3g** Fat: **14.1g**
Of which saturates: **4.9g** Fibre: **11.1g** Salt: **3.3g**

Healthy Snacks

Snacking is an easy way to accidentally indulge.

Between meals, it's all too easy to grab a packet of crisps or a chocolate bar, and that can really bump up the calories without boosting the nutrition. The healthier options in this book are delicious – and far more satisfying.

Whether you prefer dips, nibbles or a slice of toast with a tasty topping, here are some great alternatives to reaching for the biscuit tin...

Edamame Dip with Carrot Sticks

Edamame beans, also known as soya beans, are a good source of protein, which makes this dip a good post-training snack for after the gym.

Ingredients

- 150g edamame (soya) beans, frozen
- 2 tbsp low fat natural yogurt
- 1 small avocado, peeled, stoned and sliced
- ½ small red chilli
- 1 tbsp lime juice
- 10g fresh coriander
- Pinch of salt
- 2 large carrots, cut into sticks

Method

1. Put the edamame beans into boiling water for 1 minute, drain and refresh by running under the cold water tap for 30 seconds until cooled.

2. Add all of the ingredients (except the carrots) into a food processor and blend to a coarse texture. If the dip is a little too thick, loosen with a little water.

3. Serve with carrot sticks.

Preparation: 8 mins

Energy: **206 kcals** Protein: **11.5g** Carbohydrate: **17g** Of which sugars: **14g** Fat: **9.3g**
Of which saturates: **1.9g** Fibre: **8.9g** Salt: **0.3g**

Beetroot Hummus with Carrot Sticks

A great twist on a classic vegetarian dip. This hummus has all the benefits of beetroot which contains beta cyanin, a pigment that is thought to positively benefit liver function.

Ingredients

- 2 medium beetroots, peeled and cut into small chunks
- ½ x 400g can chickpeas, drained and rinsed
- 1 clove garlic, finely chopped
- ½ orange, zest only
- 2 tsp lemon juice
- ½ tsp cumin
- 1 tbsp olive oil
- Pinch of salt
- Pinch of ground black pepper
- 2 large carrots, cut into sticks

Preparation: 5 mins
Cooking: 20 mins

Method

1. Preheat the oven to 180°C / gas mark 4.
2. Place the beetroot chunks on a piece of foil and pull the edges up together and seal to make a parcel, then place on a baking tray and cook for about 20 minutes until tender. Once cooked, remove from the oven and allow to cool.
3. Place the cooled beetroot in a food processor with the chickpeas, garlic, orange zest, lemon juice, cumin and olive oil and blend until the desired consistency. If you like your hummus smooth then you may need to add a little water to thin the mixture.
4. Season to taste, and serve in a small dish with the carrot sticks.

Energy: 221 kcals Protein: 8.6g Carbohydrate: 31.4g Of which sugars: 18.2g Fat: 7.7g
Of which saturates: 1.1g Fibre: 10.7g Salt: 0.4g

Tahini Dip

Preparation: 4 mins
Cooking: 2 mins

Tahini is made from sesame seeds which are a rich source of calcium.

Ingredients

- 2 tbsp tahini
- 1 tbsp lemon juice
- Pinch of smoked paprika
- Pinch of salt
- 2 large wholemeal pitta breads

Method

1. Combine the tahini, lemon juice, paprika and salt together in a bowl.
2. Lightly toast the pitta breads, cut into strips, then serve with the dip.

Energy: 311 kcals Protein: 10.0g Carbohydrate: 30.9g Of which sugars: 2.7g Fat: 16.1g
Of which saturates: 2.4g Fibre: 6.6g Salt: 0.8g

Soya Beans with Lime and Chilli

Foods containing soya have been shown to help reduce cholesterol levels.

Ingredients

- 120g soya beans, frozen
- 1 tbsp pumpkin seeds
- 2 sticks celery, finely sliced
- 1 large spring onion, finely sliced
- ½ small red chilli, finely chopped
- 10g coriander, finely chopped
- 2 tsp low sodium soy sauce
- 1 tsp sesame oil
- 2 tsp lime juice

Method

1. Place the soya beans in a colander and run under cold water for a few minutes to defrost.

2. Set a small frying pan over a medium heat and toast the seeds for 2 minutes. Do not leave the pan as the seeds can quickly burn.

3. Place the beans in a mixing bowl and add the celery, spring onion, chilli, coriander, soy sauce, sesame oil and lime juice. Combine well and serve.

Preparation: 5 mins
Cooking: 2 mins

Kale Crisps

These vegetable crisps are low in calories considering the large serving size. You can make these in large batches and store in an airtight container for a few days (but make sure they are completely cooled before storing).

Ingredients

- 200g fresh or ready-prepared kale
- 1 tbsp olive oil
- 1 tsp smoked paprika
- ¼ tsp salt

Method

1. Preheat the oven to 180°C / gas mark 4.
2. Remove the stalks from the kale using scissors or a sharp knife. Fresh kale leaves will give you bigger crisps than the pre-packaged ready sliced variety.
3. Wash the kale then dry completely (this is really important so use kitchen towel if necessary).
4. Place the kale in a large mixing bowl with the oil and rub the leaves until coated.
5. Spread the leaves across a baking tray lined with greaseproof paper being careful not to overlap (you may need to do two batches).
6. Cook for 10 minutes until the edges have coloured and leaves are crispy. Make sure to keep your eye on them as they will burn very easily.
7. Remove from the oven and sprinkle with smoked paprika and salt.

Preparation: 5 mins
Cooking: 10 mins

Energy: 87 kcals Protein: 3.6g Carbohydrate: 1.9g Of which sugars: 1.3g Fat: 7.3g
Of which saturates: 1.0g Fibre: 4.2g Salt: 0.6g

Cashew Nut and Cacao Milk

Both cashew nuts and cacao powder are a very rich source of magnesium. A single serving of this milk provides nearly half the amount of magnesium an adult needs daily.

Ingredients

- 75g plain cashew nuts
- 2 tbsp raw cacao powder or cocoa powder
- 1 tbsp honey
- ½ vanilla pod
- Pinch of sea salt

Method

1. Soak cashews in water for 3 hours or overnight.
2. Drain cashews and add to the blender with 400ml of water.
3. Add remaining ingredients and blend for a minute on high or until completely smooth. You may want to add a little more honey for sweetness.
4. Chill for one hour before serving.

Preparation: 3 mins
(plus 3 hours soaking and 1 hour chilling)

Energy: **254 kcals** Protein: **8.2g** Carbohydrate: **16.3g** Of which sugars: **10.6g** Fat: **17.7g** Of which saturates: **4.8g** Fibre: **3.7g** Salt: **0.5g**

Miso Soup with Tofu

Preparation: 5 mins
Cooking: 10 mins

Miso soup is low in calories and makes a nourishing snack, especially with the addition of tofu.

Ingredients

- 1 sheet nori (seaweed), sliced into strips
- 3 tbsp white miso paste
- 1 large spring onion, finely sliced
- 60g firm tofu, cut into small cubes
- 1 tsp low sodium light soy sauce (optional)

Method

1. Boil 800ml of water in a saucepan and add the nori. Turn the heat down and simmer for 5 minutes.
2. Place the miso paste in a dish with a little hot water and whisk with a fork. Add this to the pan along with the spring onion and tofu. Simmer for 5 minutes.
3. Serve in bowls and season with a little soy sauce if you like.

Energy: **85 kcals** Protein: **6.7g** Carbohydrate: **5.2g** Of which sugars: **1.6g** Fat: **3.6g** Of which saturates: **0.6g** Fibre: **4.0g** Salt: **2.1g**

Avocado, Chilli and Lime on Toast

Olive oil contains a compound called oleocanthal which has been shown to have anti-inflammatory properties.

Ingredients

- 2 medium avocados, peeled and stoned
- 1 small red chilli, finely chopped
- 10g fresh coriander, finely chopped
- 1 tsp lime juice
- Pinch of salt
- Pinch of ground black pepper
- 2 slices wholemeal or granary sliced bread
- 2 tsp olive oil

Method

1. Put the avocado flesh into a small bowl.
2. Add the chilli, coriander, lime juice, salt and pepper to the avocado then combine by gently mashing with a fork.
3. Toast the bread, and then drizzle each slice with the olive oil.
4. Top the two slices of toast with the avocado mixture and serve.

Preparation: 5 mins
Cooking: 5 mins

Energy: **209 kcals** Protein: **5.1g** Carbohydrate: **14.5g** Of which sugars: **5.8g** Fat: **15.0g**
Of which saturates: **3.1g** Fibre: **4.7g** Salt: **0.3g**

Satisfying Carbs

Starchy foods like pasta, potatoes, rice and cereals are an important source of carbohydrate, and are a crucial part of a healthy diet.

These energy-rich foods are not just fuel for endurance athletes – they are also loved by the rest of us...

Wholewheat Spaghetti with Cherry Tomatoes

This simple recipe uses few ingredients and produces a delicious light meal option. This recipe contains olive oil, which is praised for its many health benefits – including promoting good heart health.

Ingredients

- 150g wholewheat spaghetti
- 2 tbsp olive oil
- 1 small red onion, finely diced
- 3 cloves garlic, crushed
- 16 cherry tomatoes, halved
- ½ medium lemon, zest only
- Pinch of salt
- Pinch of ground black pepper
- 5g fresh parsley or coriander, finely chopped

Method

1. Place spaghetti in large pan of boiling water and cook for 10 to 12 minutes, or according to packet instructions, until tender.

2. While the spaghetti is cooking, heat the oil in a deep-sided frying pan over a medium heat.

3. Add the onion and garlic, cooking for 3 minutes until softened.

4. Add the tomatoes and lemon zest, then season with salt and pepper.

5. Cook for about 5 minutes or until the tomatoes become really soft and the oil has begun to take on an orange colour.

6. Once cooked, remove from the heat.

7. When the spaghetti is cooked, drain and add it to the tomatoes, along with the chopped herbs.

8. Stir to combine, then serve.

Energy: **392 kcals** Protein: **12.5g** Carbohydrate: **58.6g** Of which sugars: **9.5g** Fat: **13.6g**
Of which saturates: **2.1g** Fibre: **11.5g** Salt: **0.3g**

Wholewheat Pasta with Chilli and Rocket

Opting for wholewheat pasta instead of white pasta will increase the amount of fibre in your diet, helping to aid digestion and protect against certain cancers.

Ingredients

- 200g wholewheat pasta
- 2 tbsp olive oil
- 2 cloves garlic, finely sliced
- 1 medium red chilli, finely sliced
- 150g rocket
- 1 tbsp lemon juice
- Pinch of salt
- Pinch of ground black pepper

Method

1. Boil a large pan of water and add the pasta. Cook according to the packet instructions.

2. Heat the oil in a large, deep-sided frying pan and add the garlic and chilli. Cook gently for 2 minutes before adding the rocket. Cook for a further 2 minutes until the rocket has wilted, then add the lemon juice, salt and pepper.

3. Take the pan off the heat, stir through the pasta and serve.

Preparation: 5 mins
Cooking: 12 mins

Energy: **345 kcals** Protein: **15.6g** Carbohydrate: **68g** Of which sugars: **4.7g** Fat: **3.1g**
Of which saturates: **0.6g** Fibre: **12.6g** Salt: **0.5g**

Broccoli and Blue Cheese Pasta Bake

Green vegetables are a great source of beta-carotene, an antioxidant that is converted to vitamin A in the body and helps to maintain a strong immune system.

Ingredients

For the pasta:
- 120g wholewheat penne pasta

- For the topping:
- 150g broccoli, cut into small florets
- 25g breadcrumbs
- 20g vegetarian Italian-style hard cheese

For the sauce:
- 25g unsalted butter
- 25g plain flour
- 250ml semi-skimmed milk
- 50g vegetarian blue cheese
- 1 tbsp Dijon mustard
- Pinch of ground black pepper

For the salad:
- 80g salad leaves
- 1 tbsp lemon juice
- 1 tsp olive oil

Method

1. Preheat the oven to 180°C / gas mark 4.

2. Bring a large saucepan of water to the boil and add the pasta. Cook for 12 minutes, or according to packet instructions, and drain.

3. In a separate saucepan, cook the broccoli florets in boiling water for 1 to 2 minutes. Then drain and plunge the broccoli into cold water to stop it overcooking.

4. In a medium heavy-bottomed pan, melt the butter over a low heat, then add the flour, stirring until it forms a paste. Stir for a minute until the flour turns a sandy texture and colour. Gradually add the milk, stirring well. Simmer until the sauce thickens to a rich consistency.

5. Add the blue cheese, mustard and pepper to the sauce and stir through.

6. Add the pasta and broccoli to the sauce and stir until coated.

7. Transfer the broccoli and pasta mixture to an ovenproof ceramic dish. Sprinkle with breadcrumbs and the vegetarian Italian-style hard cheese, then bake until the top is golden brown.

8. Serve with salad leaves dressed with lemon juice and olive oil.

Energy: **614 kcals** Protein: **26.8g** Carbohydrate: **69.9g** Of which sugars: **11.5g** Fat: **25.6g** Of which saturates: **15.2g** Fibre: **10.1g** Salt: **2.3g**

Gnocchi with Lemon and Kale Pesto

Gnocchi is made from potato and makes a great alternative to pasta. Kale is often hailed for its high concentration of minerals, including calcium.

Ingredients

- 2 tbsp pine nuts
- 1 clove garlic, crushed
- 25g fresh flat leaf parsley, finely chopped
- 50g kale, stalks removed and discarded, finely chopped
- 2 tbsp vegetarian Italian-style hard cheese, grated
- 1 medium lemon, juice and zest
- 2 tbsp olive oil
- Pinch of ground black pepper
- 400g gnocchi

Method

1. Place the pine nuts into a small frying pan and cook over a gentle heat, stirring from time to time, until evenly browned.

2. Make the pesto by mixing the garlic, parsley, kale, pine nuts, cheese and lemon zest together in a small bowl. Season with the pepper to taste and stir in the olive oil and lemon juice. Set aside.

3. Cook the gnocchi according to the packet instructions, then drain well.

4. Put the gnocchi in a serving bowl, add the pesto, stir through and serve.

Preparation: 10 mins
Cooking: 12 mins

Energy: **559 kcals** Protein: **15.5g** Carbohydrate: **66.7g** Of which sugars: **3.1g** Fat: **25.9g** Of which saturates: **3.8g** Fibre: **6g** Salt: **2.4g**

Gnocchi with Spinach, Red Pepper and Tomato Sauce

This dish provides a rich source of B vitamins that are required by the body to convert food into energy.

Ingredients

- 1 tbsp olive oil
- 1 small onion, finely diced
- 1 clove garlic, crushed
- 1 large red pepper, seeds removed and discarded, diced
- 1 x 227g can chopped tomatoes
- Pinch of salt
- 200g spinach
- 400g gnocchi

Method

1. Heat the oil in a large frying pan, then add the onion, garlic and pepper and cook gently for 5 minutes.

2. Add the tomatoes and salt then simmer for 10 to 15 minutes, stirring occasionally, until the sauce has thickened. Stir through the spinach, allowing it to wilt.

3. Meanwhile, boil the gnocchi according to packet instructions.

4. Drain the gnocchi then add it to the pan with the sauce, stirring until the gnocchi is coated in sauce.

5. Divide into two bowls and serve.

Energy: **434 kcals** Protein: **13.9g** Carbohydrate: **75.4g** Of which sugars: **13.2g** Fat: **8.7g**
Of which saturates: **1g** Fibre: **11.3g** Salt: **2.7g**

Pearl Barley Risotto with Feta Cheese

Pearl barley is a nice alternative to the traditional rice used to make risotto. Tomatoes (especially when cooked or processed) are rich in the antioxidant lycopene, which is often associated with men's health.

Ingredients

For the risotto:
- 1 tbsp olive oil
- 1 stick celery, finely sliced
- 1 small onion, finely sliced
- 2 cloves garlic, finely sliced
- ½ tsp smoked paprika
- 1 bay leaf
- 350ml low sodium vegetable stock
- 150ml passata
- 1 x 227g can chopped tomatoes
- 100g pearl barley, rinsed
- ½ medium lemon, zest only

For the topping:
- 1 tbsp caraway seeds
- 100g vegetarian feta cheese, cut into small cubes
- 1 tsp dried oregano
- 1 tbsp olive oil

Preparation: 10 mins
Cooking: 50 mins

Method

1. Heat 1 tbsp of olive oil in a thick-bottomed saucepan then add the celery, onion and garlic and cook over a low heat for 5 minutes.

2. Add the paprika, bay leaf, stock, passata and tomatoes to the pan. Stir to combine.

3. Add the pearl barley and simmer gently for 45 minutes until the barley is tender and the liquid is nearly absorbed, stirring now and then to stop the risotto sticking. Add a little extra water to the pan during cooking if the risotto starts to become too dry.

4. While the risotto is cooking, prepare the topping by toasting the caraway seeds in a small, dry pan over a low heat. Once toasted, remove the pan from the heat and leave the seeds to cool before lightly crushing.

5. In a small bowl combine the caraway seeds, feta cheese, oregano and olive oil.

6. When the risotto is cooked, stir in the lemon zest. Divide the risotto between two bowls, add the feta cheese topping and serve.

Jamaican Rice and Peas with Spring Greens

Combining rice with peas (which in the case of this dish are actually beans) makes the protein in this dish complete, meaning it contains all of the essential amino acids.

Ingredients

For the rice and peas:
- 1 tbsp extra virgin coconut oil
- 1 large red pepper, seeds removed and discarded, cut into squares
- 1 small onion, finely diced
- 175g long grain brown rice
- 200ml coconut milk
- 150ml water
- 1 tsp dried thyme
- Pinch of ground black pepper
- 1 x 400g can red kidney beans, drained and rinsed

For the greens:
- ½ tbsp extra virgin coconut oil
- 160g spring greens, finely shredded
- ½ tsp yellow mustard seeds

Method

1. Heat 1 tbsp of coconut oil in a medium saucepan, then fry the pepper and onion until they are softened and slightly brown.

2. Stir the rice into the pepper and onion mixture to coat it with the oil. Add the coconut milk, water, thyme and black pepper. Bring to the boil, cover and simmer over a very low heat for 30 minutes.

3. At the end of the 30 minutes, put the kidney beans on top of the rice without stirring, and cook for a further 15 minutes until all of the water has been absorbed.

4. While the rice and beans are cooking, prepare the greens by plunging them into boiling water. Cook for about 5 minutes, then drain.

5. Heat ½ tbsp of coconut oil in a large frying pan, add the mustard seeds and cook for 1 minute, then stir in the greens. Cook for 2 minutes until tender.

6. Divide the rice and beans onto two plates with the spring greens on the side, and serve.

Preparation: 15 mins
Cooking: 50 mins

Energy: **640 kcals** Protein: **20.5g** Carbohydrate: **66.7g** Of which sugars: **13.1g** Fat: **18.7g** Of which saturates: **13.5g** Fibre: **19.3g** Salt: **0.1g**

Twice-Baked Potatoes with Leeks and Cheese

Potatoes are a good source of B vitamins and vitamin C, both of which are essential for healthy skin.

Ingredients

- 2 large baking potatoes
- 1 medium leek
- 1 tbsp pumpkin seeds
- 80g vegetarian cream cheese with garlic and herbs
- 1 tbsp semi-skimmed milk
- Pinch of ground black pepper
- 40g vegetarian mature Cheddar cheese, coarsely grated

Preparation: 10 mins
Cooking: 80 mins

Method

1. Preheat the oven to 180°C / gas mark 4. Bake the potatoes until cooked through, approximately 45 to 60 minutes.

2. When the potatoes have nearly finished baking, prepare the leek by slicing it almost in half lengthways, then fan it out under a running tap to wash away any trapped dirt. Slice each half into four lengthways, then cut into 5mm slices.

3. Blanch the leek by plunging into a pan of boiling water for 1 minute. Drain and set aside.

4. Toast the pumpkin seeds in a dry pan over a low heat for a couple of minutes, watching them carefully so they do not burn. Set aside.

5. Once the potatoes have finished baking, cut them in half lengthways and scoop out the flesh into a bowl. Retain the potato skins for later.

6. Add the cream cheese and milk to the bowl with the potato flesh, season with black pepper, and mix together with a fork.

7. Fill each of the four potato skins with the potato and cheese mixture, then top first with the leeks, followed by the grated Cheddar cheese.

8. Place the potatoes on a baking tray and return to the oven for 20 minutes or until golden brown.

9. Sprinkle the potatoes with pumpkin seeds and serve.

Energy: 434 kcals Protein: 21.5g Carbohydrate: 49.3g Of which sugars: 5.1g Fat: 15.7g
Of which saturates: 7.6g Fibre: 7.6g Salt: 0.9g

Nourishing Veggies

There are few food groups that can boast the range of colours, shapes, textures and flavours as vegetables. This section is a celebration of these amazing foods.

From stews and curries to stuffed veggies, the following recipes are packed with mouth-watering yet health-conscious dishes to delight the most discerning of palates...

Courgette Linguini with Bean and Tomato Sauce

Replacing pasta with courgette linguini is a clever way to reduce the calorie content of this dish, as well as adding another portion of vegetables to your daily intake.

Ingredients

- 4 large courgettes
- 2 tbsp olive oil
- 2 cloves garlic, finely chopped
- ½ small red chilli, finely chopped
- 1 tbsp capers, rinsed
- 40g black olives, pitted and chopped
- ½ x 400g can cannellini beans, drained and rinsed
- 1 x 227g can chopped tomatoes
- 2 tbsp tomato purée
- 10g flat leaf parsley, finely chopped

Preparation: 20 mins
Cooking: 10 mins

Method

1. Prepare the courgette linguini by peeling lengthways with a julienne peeler to create long thin strips, then set aside.

2. In a large, non-stick, deep-sided frying pan, heat the oil over a medium heat and add the garlic. Cook very gently so as not to burn or discolour the garlic.

3. Add the chilli, capers and olives, cooking for 1 minute.

4. Add the cannellini beans, chopped tomatoes and tomato purée, cook for another 5 minutes then take off the heat and stir through the parsley.

5. Bring a large pan of water to the boil.

6. Place the courgette linguini in the pan of water and boil for 30 seconds then drain.

7. Put the drained courgettes into two bowls and top each with the bean and tomato sauce before serving.

Stuffed Peppers with Red Rice and Tomato Sauce

All peppers are rich in vitamins A, C, and K. Antioxidant vitamins A and C help to prevent cell damage. Vitamin K promotes proper blood clotting and strengthens bones.

Ingredients

For the stuffed peppers:
- 2 large yellow peppers, seeds removed and discarded, cut in half lengthways, stalk left on
- 80g red or brown rice
- 2 tbsp pine nuts
- 2 tsp olive oil
- 1 medium red onion, finely diced
- 1 clove garlic, finely chopped
- Pinch of ground cinnamon
- Pinch of allspice
- 4 dried apricots, sliced
- 2 tbsp sultanas
- 5g parsley, finely chopped
- 5g mint, finely chopped
- 2 large spring onions, sliced
- 30g vegetarian feta cheese

For the sauce:
- ½ small red chilli
- 4 medium tomatoes
- 1 clove garlic
- 1 small onion
- 5g fresh parsley
- ½ tsp ground cumin
- Pinch of salt
- Pinch of ground black pepper

Method

1. Preheat the oven to 180°C / gas mark 4.
2. Place the peppers, cut side down, on a baking sheet lined with greaseproof paper and cook for 15 minutes until tender and slightly coloured. Remove when the skin starts to brown slightly.
3. Meanwhile, cook the rice in boiling water for 20 minutes until tender, then drain.
4. Toast the pine nuts in a small frying pan over a low heat until golden brown. Be careful as they can burn easily. Remove from the pan and put in a small dish and set aside.
5. Using the same pan, heat the oil and add the diced red onion and the finely chopped garlic, cooking for 5 minutes until soft.
6. Add the spices and cook for 1 minute until fragrant then add the rice with a splash of water to prevent sticking and stir.
7. Take the pan off the heat and stir through the pine nuts, apricots, sultanas, herbs and spring onions.
8. Divide the rice mixture between the pepper halves, stuffing well. Crumble the feta cheese on top of each pepper and place back in the oven for 5 minutes.
9. Blend sauce ingredients together in a blender with 100ml of water, and then transfer to a small saucepan. Bring to the boil then reduce the heat and simmer for 15 minutes, adding a little water if needed.
10. Serve the peppers topped with the tomato sauce.

Preparation: 20 mins
Cooking: 40 mins

Butternut Squash Stuffed with Lentils and Spinach

Butternut squash is rich in beta-carotene, which helps to maintain healthy skin.

Ingredients

For the squash:
- 1 medium butternut squash, cut in half, seeds removed and discarded
- 25g butter
- Pinch of salt
- Pinch of ground black pepper

For the stuffing:
- 2 tsp olive oil
- 1 clove garlic, crushed
- 1 small red onion, thinly sliced
- 1 inch piece ginger, peeled and grated
- ½ tsp ground cinnamon
- ½ tsp cumin seeds
- ½ tsp paprika
- 50g sultanas
- ½ x 390g can green lentils in water
- 200g spinach, chopped

Method

1. Preheat the oven to 200°C / gas mark 6.

2. Using a sharp knife, score the flesh of the squash in a criss-cross pattern, so that the heat can get to the interior. Place the squash halves, cut sides facing upwards, into an ovenproof dish, dot with the butter and season with salt and freshly ground black pepper. Roast in the oven for about 40 minutes until cooked.

3. Meanwhile, make the stuffing by heating the oil in a frying pan, add the garlic and red onion and cook, stirring occasionally, for about 5 minutes.

4. Add the ginger, cinnamon, cumin seeds, paprika, sultanas and green lentils. Continue to cook for 10 minutes over a low heat until the flavours have combined, stirring frequently to avoid sticking.

5. Add the spinach and cook for 3 to 4 minutes or until the spinach has softened.

6. Place equal amounts of the stuffing mixture on top of each of the roasted squash halves, then return to the oven for 10 to 15 minutes to allow the squash to absorb some of the flavours. Serve immediately with any remaining juices from the stuffing pan spooned over.

Preparation: 15 mins
Cooking: 60 mins

Energy: **354 kcals** Protein: **11.6g** Carbohydrate: **46.2g** Of which sugars: **28.4g** Fat: **15.3g** Of which saturates: **7.2g** Fibre: **10.5g** Salt: **0.7g**

Moroccan Baked Aubergine with Dressing and Salad

Aubergines are low in calories and high in fibre. By partnering these purple vegetables with lentils, which adds protein, you should feel satisfyingly full after eating this dish.

Ingredients

For the aubergines:
- 2 large aubergines, sliced in half lengthways
- 1 tbsp olive oil
- Pinch of salt
- Pinch of ground black pepper
- 1 medium plum tomato, thinly sliced

For the lentils:
- 100g Puy lentils
- 2 large spring onions, finely sliced
- 2 sticks celery, finely sliced
- 30g sultanas
- 1 tsp ground cumin
- 10g fresh coriander, finely chopped
- 5g fresh mint, finely chopped
- Pinch of salt
- Pinch of ground black pepper

For the tomato and onion salad and dressing:
- 3 medium plum tomatoes, thinly sliced
- 1 small red onion, finely sliced
- 1 heaped tbsp low fat natural yogurt
- 1 tbsp lemon juice

Preparation: 15 mins
Cooking: 40 mins

Method

1. Preheat the oven to 180°C.
2. Drizzle the aubergine halves with the oil, season with salt and pepper, and place on a baking tray and cook for about 25 minutes, or until tender.
3. While the aubergines are cooking, rinse the lentils under cold running water, then place them in a saucepan with 200ml of water. Bring to the boil, then lower the heat and simmer for about 20 minutes until tender but still with a bite. As the lentils cook, check them periodically and add a little water if they begin to dry out.
4. Once the lentils are cooked, drain and transfer them to a bowl along with the spring onions, celery, sultanas, cumin, fresh coriander and mint.
5. Remove the aubergines from the oven and leave to cool slightly.
6. Once the aubergines have cooled enough to handle, scoop out the flesh, being careful not to pierce the skins. Add the aubergine flesh to the bowl with the lentil mixture, stir to combine, then season with salt and pepper.
7. Spoon the lentil and aubergine mixture back into the aubergine skins, then place a few tomato slices on top of each aubergine.
8. Put the aubergines back in the oven for 5 minutes.
9. To make the tomato salad, arrange the three sliced tomatoes and finely sliced red onion on a plate to serve separately.
10. Combine the yogurt and lemon juice to make the dressing.
11. Remove the aubergines from the oven and serve with the tomato salad and dressing.

Cauliflower, Potato and Spinach Curry

Including plenty of dried spices in food is a good way to add iron to your diet. This essential mineral helps to maintain healthy red blood cells.

Ingredients

- 2 tbsp olive oil
- 1 large onion, finely chopped
- 2 cloves garlic, finely chopped
- 1 tsp ground ginger
- ½ tsp turmeric
- 1 tbsp medium curry powder
- 1 x 227g can chopped tomatoes
- 1 small cauliflower, cut into small florets
- 1 large potato, peeled and cut into medium chunks
- ½ medium lemon, zest only
- Pinch of salt
- Pinch of ground black pepper
- 90g spinach
- 10g fresh coriander, roughly chopped
- 2 large wholemeal chapati

Preparation: 15 mins
Cooking: 45 mins

Method

1. Heat the oil in deep-sided frying pan over a medium heat.

2. Add the onion and garlic, cooking for 10 minutes until soft.

3. Add the ginger, turmeric and curry powder. Cook for 1 minute until the spices become darker and fragrant.

4. Stir in the tomatoes and then add the cauliflower, potato and lemon zest.

5. Cover the pan and leave to cook for 30 minutes, adding a little water as necessary, although this curry should be fairly dry.

6. Take the curry off the heat and season to taste with a little salt and pepper. (Please note: many curry powders already contain salt.)

7. Stir through the spinach until it wilts, then add the coriander.

8. Serve with wholemeal chapati.

Energy: **445 kcals** Protein: **14.6g** Carbohydrate: **59.8g** Of which sugars: **13.9g** Fat: **18.1g** Of which saturates: **2.5g** Fibre: **8.9g** Salt: **0.6g**

Winter Vegetable Curry with Raita and Brown Rice

Preparation: 20 mins
Cooking: 50 mins

This dish is a fantastic source of iron, providing 40% of your recommended daily intake.

Ingredients

- 25g flaked almonds
- 1 tbsp olive oil
- 1 small onion, finely diced
- 3 cloves garlic, crushed
- 1 inch piece ginger, peeled and finely grated
- ½ small butternut squash, peeled, seeds removed and discarded, cut into cubes
- 2 small carrots, peeled and cut into sticks
- 1 medium parsnip, peeled and cut into sticks
- 1 heaped tbsp curry paste
- 10g coriander, finely chopped
- 4 medium tomatoes, cut into quarters
- 100g brown basmati rice
- 3 tbsp low fat natural yogurt
- 50g cucumber, grated

Method

1. Toast the almonds by placing in a small frying pan over a very low heat and stirring until they are golden brown, taking care not to burn them. Put them to one side.

2. Heat the oil in a large thick-based saucepan with a lid. Add the onion, garlic and ginger and cook until soft, but not browned, for approximately 5 minutes. Stir in the squash, carrots and parsnip, and cook for a further 5 minutes until they begin to soften. Add the curry paste and cook for another 5 minutes.

3. Add 200ml of boiling water and half the coriander, cover with a lid and simmer for 40 minutes or until the vegetables are tender. Uncover, stir through the tomatoes and then simmer to reduce the sauce to a thicker consistency.

4. Meanwhile, cook the rice in a medium-sized pan of water for around 20 minutes until tender.

5. To make the raita, mix the yogurt and grated cucumber in a small bowl.

6. Garnish the curry with the remaining coriander and toasted almonds and serve with the rice and raita.

Energy: **512 kcals** Protein: **14.6g** Carbohydrate: **75.4g** Of which sugars: **24.6g** Fat: **18.5g**
Of which saturates: **2.4g** Fibre: **10.7g** Salt: **0.8g**

Thai Green Vegetable Curry with Quinoa

Quinoa is a versatile grain that makes a great alternative to rice. It also contains all of the essential amino acids your body needs.

Ingredients

- 100g quinoa
- 80g soya beans, frozen
- 2 tsp extra virgin coconut oil
- 1 clove garlic, crushed
- 1 inch piece ginger, peeled and cut into fine strips
- 1 tbsp vegetarian Thai green curry paste
- 1 small aubergine, diced into 1cm pieces
- 1 tsp lime juice
- 1 tsp soft brown sugar
- 1 or 2 tsp low sodium light soy sauce
- 1 small red pepper, seeds removed and discarded, cut into strips
- 2 large spring onions, sliced
- 100g French beans, cut into 1cm pieces
- 100g broccoli, cut into 1cm pieces
- 200ml reduced fat coconut milk
- 10g fresh coriander, finely chopped

Preparation: 15 mins
Cooking: 25 mins

Method

1. Rinse the quinoa, add it to a medium-sized saucepan of cold water and bring to the boil. Cook for a further 5 minutes or until the seeds start to 'burst' and are tender. Drain the quinoa and set aside.

2. Blanch the frozen soya beans in a pan of boiling water for 3 minutes, drain, then rinse under cold water and set aside.

3. Heat the extra virgin coconut oil in a non-stick, deep-sided frying pan or wok and add the garlic and ginger. Cook for a few minutes to flavour the oil.

4. Add the curry paste to the pan and stir for a minute until the paste becomes fragrant, then add the aubergine and cook for a further 2 minutes.

5. Add 150ml water and continue to cook for a further 5 to 8 minutes until the aubergine is tender.

6. Stir in the lime juice, sugar and 1 teaspoon of soy sauce. Taste, checking that the sauce is not too salty, then add the additional teaspoon of soy sauce if necessary.

7. Add the remaining vegetables, including the soya beans, and cook for 3 to 5 minutes until the vegetables become tender.

8. Stir through the coconut milk then remove the pan from the heat.

9. Add the coriander.

10. Spoon the quinoa into two bowls and top with curry.

Energy: **423 kcals** Protein: **18.6g** Carbohydrate: **45.6g** Of which sugars: **16.9g** Fat: **19.2g** Of which saturates: **11.8g** Fibre: **12g** Salt: **0.6g**

Gujarati Cabbage with Rice

This dish is delicious served with a portion of lentil and tomato dal (turn to page 109 for the recipe).

Ingredients

- 100g brown basmati rice
- 250g parsnips, scrubbed and cut into chunks
- 1 tbsp olive oil
- 1 clove garlic, finely chopped
- 1 tsp black mustard seeds
- 1 tsp cumin seeds
- 1 medium pointed (sweetheart) cabbage, finely shredded
- 1 small red chilli, finely chopped (discard the seeds if a milder flavour is preferred)
- Pinch of salt
- 1 tbsp lemon juice
- 1 tbsp desiccated coconut
- Fresh coriander, coarsely chopped

Method

1. Bring a medium saucepan of water to the boil and add the rice. Cook for about 20 minutes, or according to packet instructions, until tender and then drain.

2. While the rice is simmering, cook the parsnips in a pan of gently boiling water for 7 minutes until tender. Drain well and return to the pan, then lightly crush the parsnips with the back of a fork, just to break, not to mash. Set aside.

3. Heat the oil in a large frying pan, then add the garlic, mustard seeds and cumin seeds. Cook for a few minutes until the mustard seeds start to pop.

4. Add the cabbage, chilli and a pinch of salt and stir-fry for 3 to 4 minutes.

5. Add the warm parsnips to the pan and cook for a further 2 to 3 minutes until the cabbage is tender but still has some bite.

6. Stir in the lemon juice, coconut and coriander.

7. Serve with the cooked brown basmati rice and lentil and tomato dal (p109).

Preparation: 10 mins
Cooking: 25 mins

Energy: **594 kcals** Protein: **18.7g** Carbohydrate: **96.8g** Of which sugars: **22.2g** Fat: **17.6g**
Of which saturates: **8.2g** Fibre: **21g** Salt: **0.7g**

Butternut Squash Stew with Curly Kale

Kale is a good non-dairy source of calcium, and this dish provides one-third of the recommended daily intake of this important nutrient.

Ingredients

For the stew:
- 2 tbsp olive oil
- 1 medium onion, finely diced
- 1 clove garlic, finely chopped
- 1 carrot, finely diced
- ½ tsp turmeric
- ½ tsp ground cinnamon
- ½ tsp ground ginger
- 50g red lentils
- 250ml passata
- 350g butternut squash, peeled, seeds removed and discarded, cubed
- ½ x 400g can black-eyed beans, drained and rinsed
- 750ml low sodium vegetable stock
- 80g kale, washed and finely shredded
- Pinch of salt
- Pinch of pepper

To serve:
- 2 slices wholemeal baguette

Method

1. Heat the oil in a large saucepan over a medium heat.
2. Add the onions, garlic and carrots and cook for about 5 minutes, until softened.
3. Stir in the turmeric, cinnamon and ginger and continue to cook for another minute until the spices become fragrant.
4. Turn the heat down to low and add in the lentils and passata, cooking for a further 15 minutes and stirring occasionally. (You may need to add a little more passata or water during cooking.)
5. Add the squash, black-eyed beans and stock to the pan, then simmer for 30 minutes until the squash is tender.
6. Once the squash has been cooking for 20 minutes, steam the kale for about 10 minutes, either over the stew or in a separate pan, until slightly softened but still bright green.
7. Stir the kale into the squash and lentil mixture, then season to taste with a bit of salt and pepper.
8. Serve on its own or with slices of crusty wholemeal baguette.

Energy: **454 kcals** Protein: **22.4g** Carbohydrate: **74.8g** Of which sugars: **21.8g** Fat: **9.2g**
Of which saturates: **1.8g** Fibre: **16.6g** Salt: **2.5g**

Protein-Rich Dishes

Question: How can a vegetarian get enough protein?
Answer: Easily!

There are so many vegetarian foods that are packed with protein:
lentils, beans, Quorn, eggs, tofu – the list just goes on.

Over the next few pages are some simple-to-make powerhouse meal
ideas to inspire your inner foodie...

Warm Lentils with Mozzarella and Homemade Pesto

Lentils are a good source of zinc which helps to maintain a strong immune system.

Ingredients

For the pesto:
- 100g spinach, chopped
- 20g cashew nuts
- 2 tbsp lemon juice
- 30g fresh basil leaves, chopped

For the lentils:
- 160g Puy lentils, rinsed
- 2 tsp olive oil
- 1 large carrot, peeled and finely diced
- 2 sticks celery, finely diced
- 1 small onion, finely diced
- 1 small bulb fennel, finely sliced
- 1 clove garlic, crushed
- 2 sprigs fresh thyme, stalks removed and discarded
- Pinch of salt
- Pinch of ground black pepper
- 80g vegetarian mozzarella, torn

Preparation: 15 mins
Cooking: 25 mins

Method

1. Make the pesto by placing all of the pesto ingredients in a food processor (or blender) and blend for 1 minute. Check the consistency. The pesto should be of drizzling consistency. If it is too thick, add a little water and blend again until desired consistency is achieved. Set the pesto aside.

2. Bring a pan of water to the boil, and carefully add the lentils. Reduce the heat and cook for 15 minutes or until the lentils are tender, but still with a bite.

3. While the lentils are cooking, heat the olive oil over a medium heat in a large non-stick, deep-sided frying pan.

4. Add the carrot, celery, onion, fennel, garlic and thyme leaves, and cook for 8 to 10 minutes until the vegetables are soft. Season with a pinch of salt and pepper.

5. When the lentils have finished cooking, drain them and add to the pan with the vegetables. Add a splash of water, stir for a few minutes, then remove from the heat.

6. Divide the lentils into two bowls, topping with mozzarella and a drizzle of pesto to serve.

Energy: **523 kcals** Protein: **33.4g** Carbohydrate: **56.9g** Of which sugars: **10.3g** Fat: **18.7g** Of which saturates: **7.2g** Fibre: **17.7g** Salt: **0.8g**

Baked Black Beans and Kidney Beans with Sweet Potato Wedges

Sweet potatoes are a rich source of beta-carotene which is a powerful antioxidant that helps to maintain healthy skin.

Ingredients

- 1 small onion, finely diced
- 2 cloves garlic, finely chopped
- 1 x 400g can black beans or pinto beans, drained
- 1 x 220g can red kidney beans, drained
- 125ml low sodium vegetable stock
- 85g tomato purée
- 1 tbsp molasses
- 2 tbsp reduced sodium soy sauce
- ½ tsp ground cumin
- ½ tsp mustard powder
- 10g fresh parsley, finely chopped
- A dash of olive oil (for greasing)
- 2 medium sweet potatoes, sliced into wedges

Method

1. Preheat oven to 180°C / gas mark 4.
2. Add all the ingredients except for the sweet potato wedges to a large baking dish and mix well.
3. Bake uncovered for 45 minutes.
4. While the beans are cooking, place the sweet potato wedges on a greased baking sheet and place in the oven. Cook for about 20 minutes until tender.
5. Serve the beans in bowls accompanied by the wedges.

Mixed Bean Stew with Sliced Avocado

Beans provide one of the best sources of fibre. Fibre helps to control the release of sugar from carbohydrates, which helps maintain steady energy levels and a feeling of fullness.

Ingredients

- 1 tbsp olive oil
- 1 small onion, finely diced
- 1 clove garlic, crushed
- 1 stick celery, finely sliced
- 1 medium carrot, diced
- 1 large red pepper, seeds removed and discarded, finely diced
- ½ tsp chilli powder
- ½ tsp ground cumin
- ½ tsp smoked paprika
- ½ x 400g can black beans, drained and rinsed
- ½ x 400g can chickpeas, drained and rinsed
- 1 x 200g can sweetcorn, drained and rinsed
- ½ x 400g can chopped tomatoes
- 250ml low sodium vegetable stock
- 1 tbsp tomato purée
- 1 tbsp lime juice
- Pinch of salt
- Pinch of ground black pepper
- 1 medium avocado, peeled, stoned and sliced

Method

1. Heat the oil in a large saucepan then add the onion, garlic, celery, carrot and pepper and cook for about 10 minutes, until soft.

2. Add the chilli powder, ground cumin and smoked paprika and cook for a further 2 minutes.

3. Add the black beans, chickpeas, sweetcorn, chopped tomatoes and vegetable stock and simmer for about 20 minutes, stirring occasionally. If the stew starts to dry out, add a little water.

4. Stir in the tomato purée, lime juice, salt, pepper and cook for a further 5 minutes.

5. Serve in bowls with the slices of avocado.

Preparation: 15 mins
Cooking: 35 mins

Chickpea, Sweet Potato and Okra Tagine

Pulses provide a valuable source of fibre and are a useful source of zinc, which is essential for maintaining a strong immune system.

Ingredients

- 1 tbsp olive oil
- 1 small onion, finely chopped
- 1 clove garlic, crushed
- 1 inch piece ginger, peeled and grated
- 1 tsp ground cumin
- ½ tsp ground cinnamon
- ¼ tsp ground allspice
- 2 large sweet potatoes, peeled and cubed
- 250ml low sodium vegetable stock
- 1 x 200g can chickpeas, drained and rinsed
- 100g okra, topped and tailed and cut into 1cm pieces
- Pinch of salt
- Pinch of ground black pepper
- 100g couscous
- 10g fresh coriander, finely chopped
- 10g fresh flat leaf parsley, finely chopped

Method

1. Heat the olive oil in a medium sized saucepan for 1 minute, add the onion and cook gently without browning for 5 minutes, stirring occasionally.

2. Add the garlic, ginger and spices to the pan and cook gently for a further 2 minutes until they become fragrant.

3. Add the sweet potatoes and stock and bring to the boil, then reduce heat and simmer gently for 10 to 15 minutes, stirring occasionally until the sweet potatoes are tender.

4. Add the chickpeas and okra to the pan and cook uncovered for a further 5 minutes (adding a little water if the mixture becomes dry and sticks). Season with salt and pepper.

5. While the tagine is cooking, prepare the couscous by putting it in a bowl and covering with 150ml of boiling water. Leave it to stand for 5 minutes until tender, then stir in the fresh coriander and parsley.

6. Serve the tagine over the couscous in bowls.

Preparation: 15 mins
Cooking: 25 mins

Energy: **466 kcals** Protein: **13.5g** Carbohydrate: **87.2g** Of which sugars: **16g** Fat: **9.4g** Of which saturates: **1.5g** Fibre: **10.5g** Salt: **1.0g**

Moroccan Chickpea and Aubergine Stew

Aubergines are very low in calories and high in fibre, making them a good vegetable to include in your diet if you are looking to lose weight. You can reduce the calorie content of this dish by serving it without couscous.

Ingredients

- 1 tbsp olive oil
- 1 large onion, diced
- 1 clove garlic, finely chopped
- 1 tsp ground cumin
- 1 tsp ground coriander
- 1 large aubergine, cut into chunks
- 1 x 400g can chickpeas, drained and rinsed
- 1 x 400g can chopped tomatoes
- ½ tsp ground cinnamon
- 1 tsp harissa paste
- Pinch of salt
- 100g couscous

Method

1. Heat the oil in a large pan and gently fry the onion and garlic for 5 minutes until softened but not browned.

2. Stir in the cumin and coriander, cook for a few minutes, then add the aubergine, chickpeas, tomatoes, cinnamon, harissa paste, salt and 250ml of water.

3. Bring the stew to the boil, then lower the heat and simmer, half-covered, for about 30 minutes until the vegetables are tender and the mixture has thickened.

4. While the stew is cooking, prepare the couscous by placing it in a bowl and covering it with 150ml of boiling water. Cover the bowl with a plate or lid and leave the couscous to stand for 5 minutes, until tender.

5. Fluff the couscous with a fork, then evenly divide it between two plates. Top the couscous with stew and serve.

Energy: **566 kcals** Protein: **25.2g** Carbohydrate: **89.4g** Of which sugars: **16.2g** Fat: **12.7g**
Of which saturates: **1.3g** Fibre: **20.8g** Salt: **1.3g**

Black Bean and Quorn Mince Chilli in Taco Shells

Quorn is a great vegetarian source of protein. It is also high in zinc – one of the minerals crucial to maintaining a healthy body.

Ingredients

For the chilli:
- 2 tsp olive oil
- 1 medium onion, finely diced
- 1 clove garlic, crushed
- 1 large red pepper, seeds removed and discarded, finely chopped
- 200g Quorn mince
- 1 tsp chilli powder
- 1 tsp ground cumin
- 1 x 227g can chopped tomatoes
- 200ml low sodium vegetable stock
- ½ x 400g can black beans or kidney beans, drained and rinsed
- 4 taco shells

For the sides:
- 50g iceberg lettuce, shredded
- 1 tsp lime juice
- Pinch of salt
- 2 medium tomatoes, diced
- 50g sour cream
- 1 small avocado, peeled, stoned and sliced
- 10g fresh coriander, finely chopped

Method

1. Heat the oil in a large non-stick, deep-sided frying pan then add the onion, garlic and red pepper, cooking for 5 minutes to soften.

2. Add the Quorn mince and cook for a further 5 minutes.

3. Add the chilli powder and cumin and cook for 1 minute until the spices become fragrant.

4. Stir in the can of tomatoes and stock, and cook for 10 minutes

5. While the chilli starts to cook, preheat the oven to 180°C / gas mark 4 in preparation for the taco shells.

6. Add the beans to the chilli mixture, stir, and cook for a further 10 minutes.

7. While the chilli continues to cook, dress the lettuce with lime juice and a pinch of salt.

8. Place the taco shells on a large non-stick baking sheet and bake in the oven for 2 minutes.

9. Remove the chilli from the heat and place in a large bowl.

10. Give each person two taco shells and serve the chilli, lettuce, diced fresh tomatoes, sour cream, avocado and coriander separately to build your own tacos.

Preparation: 10 mins
Cooking: 35 mins

Energy: **604 kcals** Protein: **28g** Carbohydrate: **50.7g** Of which sugars: **18.9g** Fat: **30.8g**
Of which saturates: **8.6g** Fibre: **16.1g** Salt: **1.9g**

Beetroot and Chickpea Curry

Betacyanin, the pigment that gives beetroot its purple colour, is thought to help with liver function.

Ingredients

- 100g brown rice
- 1 tsp olive oil
- 1 small onion, finely chopped
- 2 cloves garlic, finely chopped
- 1 inch piece ginger, peeled and grated
- ½ tsp turmeric
- ½ tsp ground coriander
- ½ tsp ground cumin
- 200ml low sodium vegetable stock
- 2 medium tomatoes, chopped
- 2 medium beetroots, peeled and diced into small pieces
- 1 x 210g can chickpeas, drained and rinsed
- 1 large carrot, peeled and diced into small pieces
- ½ medium lemon, zest only, finely grated
- 200ml reduced fat coconut milk
- 10g fresh coriander, chopped

Method

1. Bring a large pan of water to the boil, add the rice and cook for 20 minutes (or according to packet instructions) until tender.

2. While the rice is cooking, heat the oil in a large deep-sided frying pan, then add the onion, cooking on a medium heat for 5 minutes.

3. Add the garlic and ginger and cook for a further 5 minutes, being careful not to burn the garlic.

4. Add the spices and cook for 1 minute until the spices become fragrant.

5. Add the stock and tomatoes, bring to the boil, then add the beetroot, chickpeas, carrot and lemon zest.

6. Reduce the heat and simmer for 15 minutes.

7. While the curry is simmering, check the rice. Once the rice is tender, drain, set aside and cover to keep warm.

8. Now, add the coconut milk to the curry and simmer for a further 5 minutes.

9. Divide the rice between two plates and top with the curry. Sprinkle with the coriander and serve.

Preparation: 10 mins
Cooking: 45 mins

Energy: **494 kcals** Protein: **15.6g** Carbohydrate: **78.3g** Of which sugars: **17.4g** Fat: **15.5g**
Of which saturates: **9.7g** Fibre: **13.7g** Salt: **1.5g**

Lentil and Tomato Dal with Wholemeal Roti Bread

Dal is a delicious way to boost your intake of fibre and minerals such as iron and zinc.

Ingredients

- 1 tbsp olive oil
- 1 medium onion, finely chopped
- 1 clove garlic, crushed
- 1 inch piece ginger, peeled and grated
- 1 large carrot, peeled and diced into small pieces
- 1 large potato, peeled and diced into small pieces
- 1 tsp ground cumin
- 100g red lentils, rinsed
- 600ml low sodium vegetable stock
- 400ml passata
- 1 x 210g can chickpeas, drained and rinsed
- 1 tbsp lemon juice
- Pinch of ground black pepper
- 1 wholemeal roti

Method

1. Heat the oil in a large saucepan. Add the onion, garlic and ginger and fry gently for 5 minutes.

2. Add the carrot, potato, cumin, lentils, stock and passata to the pan. Bring to the boil then turn heat down to a simmer. Cover the pan and cook for 20 minutes, stirring occasionally.

3. Add the chickpeas, and more water if needed, and cook for a further 20 minutes, continuing to stir from time to time.

4. Ladle the dal into bowls and top with a squeeze of lemon juice and a little black pepper.

5. Serve with wholemeal roti.

Energy: **649 kcals** Protein: **29.2g** Carbohydrate: **108.7g** Of which sugars: **25.9g** Fat: **12.9g**
Of which saturates: **6.3g** Fibre: **18g** Salt: **1.8g**

Preparation: 20 mins
Cooking: 30 mins

Mushroom, Walnut and Lentil Burgers with Sweet Potato Wedges

Sweet potatoes are ranked low on the glycaemic index (GI). Following a low GI diet has been shown to have numerous health benefits and can be a good way to control your weight.

Ingredients

For the crunchy salsa:
- 1 small yellow pepper, seeds removed and discarded, finely diced
- ½ small onion, finely diced
- 1 stick celery, finely diced
- 6 cherry tomatoes, finely chopped
- 1 tbsp lime juice
- Pinch of salt
- Pinch of ground black pepper
- ½ small red chilli, very finely diced

For the sweet potato wedges:
- 2 large sweet potatoes, peeled and cut into wedges
- 1 tbsp olive oil
- Pinch of salt
- Pinch of pepper

For the burgers:
- 2 tbsp walnuts, chopped into small pieces
- 2 tbsp olive oil
- 1 small onion, finely diced
- 2 cloves garlic, crushed
- 150g chestnut mushrooms, finely chopped
- 1 tsp smoked paprika
- ½ tsp ground cumin
- Pinch of cayenne pepper
- Pinch of salt
- Pinch of ground black pepper
- ½ x 390g can green lentils, drained and rinsed
- 10g coriander, finely chopped
- 40g store-bought or homemade wholemeal breadcrumbs

Method

1. Preheat the oven to 180°C / gas mark 4.
2. Prepare the salsa by combining the first five ingredients in a small bowl, then season to taste with salt, pepper and chilli and set aside.
3. Arrange the sweet potato wedges on a baking tray, drizzle with 1 tbsp of olive oil, season, and bake for about 20 minutes until tender.
4. For the burgers, warm a small frying pan over a medium heat, add the walnuts and toast for a few minutes, stirring occasionally. Note: walnuts burn easily. When the walnuts are toasted, set them aside to cool.
5. Heat 1 tbsp of the olive oil in a large non-stick, deep-sided frying pan over a medium heat. Add the onion and garlic and cook for 5 minutes or until softened.
6. Add the mushrooms and spices, cooking for a further 5 minutes, then season to taste. Take the pan off the heat and leave the mushrooms to cool slightly.
7. Add the mushroom mixture and lentils to a food processor and blend until smooth.
8. Transfer the mushroom and lentil mixture into a large mixing bowl then combine with the walnuts, coriander and breadcrumbs.
9. Form this mixture into two large, or four small, patties.
10. Cook the patties by heating a large non-stick frying pan over a high heat. Once hot, add the remaining olive oil and gently place the burgers into the pan.
11. Cook each side for 2 to 3 minutes or until the outside of the patties start to colour and turn crispy. Flip the burgers gently to avoid them breaking up.
12. Serve the patties hot with the crunchy salsa and the sweet potato wedges.

Energy: **504 kcals** Protein: **15.1g** Carbohydrate: **62.2g** Of which sugars: **14.5g** Fat: **23.8g** Of which saturates: **3g** Fibre: **12.2g** Salt: **0.7g**

111

Spanish Omelette

This recipe serves four, so you could eat half and save the rest to eat cold for lunch the following day. Eggs provide a good supply of B vitamins that help to convert food into energy and support a healthy nervous system.

Ingredients

- 250g waxy potatoes such as Charlotte or new potatoes, washed and sliced into ½cm thick slices
- 1 small onion, finely sliced
- 1 tbsp olive oil
- 1 small red pepper, seeds removed and discarded, finely sliced
- 4 medium free-range eggs
- Pinch of salt
- Pinch of ground black pepper
- A few chives, snipped into small pieces with scissors
- 50g frozen peas
- 100g salad leaves
- 2 tsp lemon juice

Method

1. Simmer the potato slices very gently in boiling water for about 8 minutes until just cooked through. Be careful not to overcook them. Drain.

2. Cook the onion in a medium frying pan with 2 tsp of the oil over a low heat for about 5 minutes. Add the red pepper and cook for another 5 minutes until softened.

3. Break the eggs into a bowl and beat with a whisk or fork then season with salt and pepper. Stir in the chives and the peas.

4. Heat the grill to medium.

5. Add the rest of the oil to the frying pan and add the potatoes. Pour over the egg mixture and cook gently for about 15 mins until almost set and golden brown underneath.

6. Put the frying pan under the grill. Cook for a further minute or two.

7. Turn the omelette onto a plate, cut into quarters and serve one quarter per person with salad leaves dressed in lemon juice.

Serves: 4
Preparation: 10 mins
Cooking: 20 mins

Energy: **322 kcals** Protein: **18.9g** Carbohydrate: **29.6g** Of which sugars: **8.4g** Fat: **15g**
112 Of which saturates: **4g** Fibre: **5.8g** Salt: **0.5g**

Preparation: 10 mins
Cooking: 30 mins

Shakshuka (Spiced Tomato Baked Eggs)

Eggs are a good source of iron, and this simple lunch dish provides
one-third of the recommended daily intake of this important nutrient.

Ingredients

- 1 tbsp olive oil
- ½ tsp fennel seeds
- 1 small onion, finely diced
- 1 clove garlic, finely chopped
- 1 large red pepper, seeds
  removed and discarded, cut into
  strips
- 1 tsp smoked paprika
- Pinch of saffron or turmeric
- 1 x 400g can chopped tomatoes
- Pinch of salt
- Pinch of ground black pepper
- 4 free-range eggs
- 2 medium slices wholemeal or
  granary sliced bread, toasted

Method

1. Heat the oil in a large non-stick, deep-sided frying
   pan. Add the fennel seeds and cook for 1 minute.

2. Add the onion and garlic to the pan and cook for
   another 3 minutes.

3. Add in the pepper, smoked paprika, saffron or
   turmeric, tomatoes, salt and pepper. Cook for 25
   minutes until the peppers are soft, adding more
   water as necessary to keep the mixture moist.

4. Make four small wells in the tomato and pepper
   sauce, drop in the eggs, cover the pan and cook for
   5 minutes until the whites of the egg are cooked.

5. Spoon two spicy tomato baked eggs onto each
   plate and serve with toasted bread.

Energy: 350 kcals Protein: 21.8g Carbohydrate: 32.6g Of which sugars: 14.4g Fat: 15.6g
Of which saturates: 4.0g Fibre: 7.4g Salt: 1.2g

Pea, Spinach and Goat's Cheese Frittata

This meal provides you with two of your five-a-day and is a good source of high-quality protein.

Ingredients

For the frittata:
- 3 tsp olive oil
- 1 medium red onion, thinly sliced
- 1 clove garlic, finely chopped
- 50g spinach
- 100g peas, fresh or frozen
- 6 free-range eggs
- 100ml semi-skimmed milk
- 5g chives, finely chopped
- Pinch of salt
- Pinch of ground black pepper
- 50g vegetarian goat's cheese, broken into small pieces

For the salad:
- 100g salad leaves
- 1 tsp olive oil
- 1 tbsp lemon juice

Method

1. In a non-stick frying pan, add 2 tsp of the olive oil and cook the red onion and garlic over a medium heat for 5 to 10 minutes until soft.

2. Remove the pan from the heat, transfer the onion and garlic to a small bowl.

3. Add 1 tsp of olive oil to the frying pan, turn the heat to high, then add the spinach and peas. Cook for a few minutes until the spinach has wilted, then add the cooked onion and garlic, spreading the mixture evenly to cover the base of the pan.

4. Crack the eggs into a bowl with the milk and whisk until fully combined, then add the chives, salt and pepper. Pour the egg mixture over the vegetables in the frying pan.

5. Heat the grill to medium.

6. Dot the egg mixture with pieces of goat's cheese and turn the heat down, leaving the frittata to cook until the egg starts to set.

7. Now place the pan under the grill to cook the top of the frittata until it starts to brown, approximately 10 minutes.

8. Remove the frittata from the grill and leave it to cool for a few minutes.

9. While the frittata is cooling, evenly divide the salad leaves between two plates and dress with olive oil and lemon juice.

10. Carefully slide the frittata onto a chopping board, slice and serve on the plates with the salad.

Preparation: 10 mins
Cooking: 30 mins

Energy: **480 kcals** Protein: **32.9g** Carbohydrate: **15.5g** Of which sugars: **9.9g** Fat: **32.3g**
Of which saturates: **11.2g** Fibre: **6.3g** Salt: **1.2g**

Supergreen Stir-Fry with Marinated Tofu

Choosing wholegrain varieties of rice helps to increase your daily fibre intake, which is good for a healthy digestive system. Wholegrain foods are also a good source of B vitamins which help to convert food into energy.

Ingredients

- 80g brown rice
- 20g cashew nuts
- 1 tbsp extra virgin coconut oil
- 1 medium red onion, sliced
- 2 cloves garlic, finely chopped
- 1 small red chilli, finely chopped
- 160g marinated tofu pieces
- 100g broccoli, cut into small florets
- 1 large courgette, cut into sticks
- 50g soya beans, frozen
- 10g fresh coriander, finely chopped
- 2 tsp low sodium light soy sauce

Method

1. Bring a large saucepan of water to the boil. Add the rice and cook for 20 minutes until tender.

2. While the rice is cooking, toast the cashew nuts in a small pan over a medium heat until they turn golden brown. Watch the pan carefully as the nuts can easily burn. Once browned, remove from heat.

3. Next, heat the coconut oil in a wok or large, deep-sided frying pan, add the onion, garlic and chilli and cook for 1 minute, then add the tofu and cook for a further 2 minutes.

4. Stir in the broccoli, courgette and soya beans, adding a small splash of water to the pan so the vegetables can cook in the steam. Cook for 5 minutes until the vegetables are tender, stirring in the cashew nuts halfway through.

5. Remove the pan from the heat and mix in the coriander and soy sauce.

6. Drain the rice and divide it between two bowls, then top with the stir-fry.

Preparation: 15 mins
Cooking: 30 mins

Energy: 507 kcals Protein: 26.6g Carbohydrate: 46g Of which sugars: 9.1g Fat: 24.3g
Of which saturates: 5.8g Fibre: 9.8g Salt: 1.3g

Winter Vegetable and Quorn Stir-Fry

Stir-frying is a great way to cook Brussels sprouts. These little cabbages are a source of sulphur compounds which have been associated with protecting the body from certain cancers.

Ingredients

- 120g quick-cook egg noodles
- 1 tbsp extra virgin coconut oil
- 1 small red onion, finely sliced
- 1 inch piece ginger, peeled and finely grated
- 1 clove garlic, crushed
- 1 large carrot, peeled and finely sliced
- 100g Quorn pieces
- 100g chestnut mushrooms, finely sliced
- 100g Brussels sprouts, trimmed and shredded
- 1 tbsp low sodium light soy sauce
- ½ medium lime

Method

1. Cook the noodles according to packet instructions, then drain and set aside.

2. Heat the oil in a wok or large frying pan, add the onion, ginger, garlic and carrot and cook for 2 minutes.

3. Add the Quorn, mushrooms and Brussels sprouts, then cook until the sprouts have wilted.

4. Transfer the mixture to a large bowl and set aside.

5. Return the wok to the heat, add the soy sauce and the drained noodles, and stir.

6. Return the Quorn mixture to the wok, toss well with the noodles for 1 minute to heat through, then take off the heat.

7. Divide the stir-fry into two bowls and serve with a squeeze of lime juice.

Energy: **422 kcals** Protein: **18.7g** Carbohydrate: **55.7g** Of which sugars: **8.5g** Fat: **15.4g** Of which saturates: **8.5g** Fibre: **8.6g** Salt: **1.4g**

Tofu Steak with Coconut and Lemongrass Rice

Tofu is made from soya protein and has been shown to help reduce cholesterol levels.

Ingredients

For the lemongrass rice:
- 100g brown rice
- 2 sticks lemongrass
- 150ml reduced fat coconut milk
- 50g soya beans, frozen
- 10g fresh coriander, chopped
- 2 large spring onion, finely sliced

For the dressing:
- 1½ tbsp low sodium soy sauce
- 2 tbsp mirin
- 1 tsp sesame oil

For the tofu:
- 1 tbsp cornflour
- Pinch of ground black pepper
- Pinch of salt
- 300g firm tofu
- 1 tbsp groundnut oil
- 2 tsp black sesame seeds

Preparation: 10 mins
Cooking: 40 mins

Method

1. Place the rice in a colander and rinse well.
2. Carefully bruise the lemongrass by bashing it with a rolling pin or the handle of a heavy knife.
3. Place the rice in a saucepan with 150ml water, the coconut milk and lemongrass, then bring to the boil. Reduce the heat to a gentle simmer and cook the rice for about 25 minutes or until tender, stirring occasionally. If the rice dries out add a little more coconut milk or water.
4. While the rice is cooking, you can prepare the rest of the dish. To make the dressing, combine the soy sauce, mirin and sesame oil in a small bowl using a whisk or fork.
5. Next, prepare the coating for the tofu. Place the cornflour on a small plate and season with the ground black pepper and a pinch of salt.
6. Lay the tofu onto kitchen roll and gently squeeze it dry. Cut the tofu into four pieces lengthways.
7. Coat both sides of each piece of tofu with the cornflour mixture.
8. In a large non-stick frying pan heat the groundnut oil until it begins to smoke, then place the tofu in the pan and cook each side for 3 minutes or until golden brown in colour.
9. Once the rice has cooked, remove the lemongrass and stir through the soya beans, coriander and spring onion. Set aside for 5 minutes or until the soya beans have defrosted in the hot rice.
10. To serve, split the rice between two plates and top with two slices of tofu. Drizzle the tofu with the soy dressing and sprinkle with the sesame seeds.

Marinated Ginger Tofu with Pak Choi

This dish contains half of your recommended daily intake of iron in a single serving. This mineral is essential for maintaining healthy blood. Low levels of iron can lead to tiredness and fatigue.

Ingredients

For the rice:
- 100g jasmine rice

For the marinade:
- 1 inch piece ginger, peeled and grated
- 2 tbsp low sodium light soy sauce
- 1 tbsp soft brown sugar

For the tofu:
- 250g firm tofu, drained, gently pressed by hand to remove liquid and cut into 2cm cubes
- 1 tbsp groundnut oil
- ½ inch piece ginger, peeled and finely sliced
- 250g pak choi
- 1 tbsp apple juice
- 1 tbsp rice vinegar
- ½ tsp dried chilli flakes

Preparation: 15 mins
Cooking: 15 mins

Method

1. Bring a large saucepan of water to the boil and add the rice. Cook the rice according to packet instructions. Drain, cover it to keep it warm, and set aside.

2. While the rice is cooking combine the marinade ingredients together in a bowl. Add the tofu pieces, toss together and set aside to marinate for 10 to 15 minutes.

3. Heat a non-stick wok or large frying pan over high heat and add half the groundnut oil. When the oil starts to smoke, add the ginger slices and stir-fry for a few seconds. Add the pak choi leaves and stir-fry for a further 2 minutes. Add a small splash of water to create some steam and cook for 2 minutes more until the leaves are wilting, then remove and set aside.

4. Very carefully rinse the wok under cold water and dry with kitchen towel. Reheat the wok and add the remaining oil. When it starts to smoke, add the tofu pieces (retaining the marinade) and stir-fry for 5 to 10 minutes. Toss the tofu to brown it evenly on all sides, taking care not to break it up.

5. Add the apple juice and rice vinegar to the wok then add the remaining marinade, bring to a bubble and let the liquid reduce. Sprinkle over the chilli flakes and toss well.

6. Spoon the tofu onto the pak choi and serve immediately with the jasmine rice.

Energy: **453 kcals** Protein: **22g** Carbohydrate: **52g** Of which sugars: **10.8g** Fat: **15.4g**
Of which saturates: **2.5g** Fibre: **10.3g** Salt: **1.7g**

Bulgur Wheat, Lentils and Barley with Smoked Tofu

Tofu provides a good source of complete protein in a vegetarian diet, as it contains all the essential amino acids required by the body.

Ingredients

- 1 tsp olive oil
- 100g marinated tofu pieces
- ½ tsp smoked paprika
- 1½ tsp balsamic vinegar
- 1 sachet cooked bulgur wheat, green lentils and barley
- 1 small red onion, finely sliced
- 1 roasted red pepper (from a jar)
- 80g canned artichoke hearts in water, drained and sliced
- 100g spinach

Method

1. Pour the olive oil into a small non-stick frying pan, add the tofu pieces and the smoked paprika and cook for 5 minutes.

2. Stir in the balsamic vinegar and allow to sizzle and reduce.

3. Put the bulgur wheat mixture into a bowl, add the onion and pepper and toss together gently to break up. Then add the cooked tofu and artichokes and toss again.

4. Scatter the mixture over the spinach leaves and serve.

Preparation: 10 mins
Cooking: 10 mins

Energy: **384 kcals** Protein: **21.5g** Carbohydrate: **45.85g** Of which sugars: **8.55g** Fat: **10.3g**
Of which saturates: **1.35g** Fibre: **14.3g** Salt: **1.4g**

Preparation: 15 mins
Cooking: 20 mins

Cajun Quorn with Coriander Rice and Mango Salsa

Quorn provides a good low fat source of protein as well as being a great source of zinc, which helps to maintain a strong immune system.

Ingredients

For the mango salsa:
- 1 medium ripe mango, peeled and cut into small chunks
- 5 cherry tomatoes, halved
- 5g coriander, finely chopped
- 1 small red chilli, finely chopped
- 1 tbsp lime juice
- Pinch of salt
- Pinch of ground black pepper

For the Cajun Quorn:
- 350g Quorn pieces
- ½ tbsp smoked paprika
- 1 tbsp ground cumin
- ½ tbsp ground coriander
- 1 tsp crushed dried chilli
- 1 garlic clove, crushed
- 1 tbsp olive oil

For the coriander rice:
- 100g brown rice
- 1 tsp olive oil
- 1 large spring onions, finely sliced
- 10g coriander, finely chopped

Method

1. Preheat the oven to 180°C / gas mark 4.

2. Bring a saucepan of water to the boil and add the brown rice. Lower the heat, cover, and cook for about 20 minutes until the rice is tender. Drain and set aside.

3. Make the salsa by combining all of the ingredients in a bowl and set aside.

4. In a plastic freezer bag add the Quorn pieces, paprika, ground cumin, ground coriander, dried chilli, garlic and olive oil. Shake the bag until the Quorn is completely coated in the spice mixture.

5. Transfer the spiced, coated Quorn pieces to a large, non-stick baking tray and bake in the preheated oven for 10 minutes until lightly browned. Remove from the oven and set aside.

6. Combine the cooked rice with the olive oil, spring onions and coriander.

7. Serve the Cajun Quorn with the rice and mango salsa.

Ghanaian Red Stew

Brown rice scores low on the glycaemic index (GI), meaning it has less effect on your blood sugar levels than white rice. It also helps to control hunger pangs.

Ingredients

- 1 tbsp olive oil
- 1 medium plantain or very firm banana, thinly sliced
- 1 small onion, chopped
- 1 clove garlic, chopped
- 1 inch piece ginger, peeled and grated
- ½ small red chilli, chopped
- 200ml passata
- 100ml reduced sodium vegetable stock
- 1 tsp soft brown sugar
- ½ x 400g can black-eyed beans, drained and rinsed
- 100g brown rice
- 200g marinated tofu pieces
- 10g fresh parsley, chopped
- Pinch of salt
- Pinch of ground black pepper

Method

1. Heat half of the oil in a large non-stick pan over a medium heat and fry the plantain or banana until golden brown, then put to one side.

2. Heat the remaining oil in a large saucepan on a medium heat and fry the onion for 5 to 10 minutes, or until softened. Add the garlic, ginger, chilli, passata, vegetable stock, sugar and black-eyed beans. Bring to the boil then reduce the heat and simmer for 25 to 30 minutes.

3. While the stew is cooking, bring a saucepan of water to the boil and then add the rice. Cook for about 20 minutes or until tender, then drain and set aside.

4. Stir the tofu and parsley into the stew, season with the salt and pepper, then continue to cook for 5 minutes.

5. Serve the stew with the slices of plantain or banana and rice.

Preparation: 15 mins
Cooking: 50 mins

Energy: **462.5 kcals** Protein: **23g** Carbohydrate: **56.45g** Of which sugars: **9g** Fat: **17.25g**
Of which saturates: **2.6g** Fibre: **5.5g** Salt: **2.6g**

Avocado and Refried Bean Burrito-Style Wrap

This Mexican-inspired dish is rich in fibre, which helps to maintain good heart health and digestion.

Ingredients

- 50g brown rice
- 50g iceberg lettuce, finely sliced
- 1 large spring onion, finely sliced
- 1 medium tomato, chopped
- ½ x 200g can sweetcorn, drained
- ½ small red chilli, finely sliced
- 10g coriander, finely chopped
- 1 tbsp lime juice
- Pinch of salt
- 2 large wholemeal wraps
- 1 x 215g can refried beans
- 1 small avocado, peeled, stoned and sliced
- 30g vegetarian Cheddar cheese, grated

Method

1. Bring a medium saucepan of water to the boil. Add the brown rice to the pan and cook for about 20 minutes until tender. Drain and then run under cold water to cool.

2. To make the salad filling, put the lettuce, spring onion, tomato, sweetcorn, chilli, coriander, lime juice and salt in a bowl and combine well.

3. Lay the wraps out flat and spread with the refried beans then sprinkle with the cooked rice.

4. Place the avocado slices on top of the refried beans and rice and then add the salad.

5. Sprinkle with the cheese and then roll and cut each burrito in half to serve.

Energy: **560 kcals** Protein: **20.4g** Carbohydrate: **74g** Of which sugars: **6.7g** Fat: **18.8g**
Of which saturates: **6.1g** Fibre: **14.3g** Salt: **2.4g**

Desserts and Sweet Treats

We all know a little bit of what you love does you good. But did you know that there is a way you can get all the sweet enjoyment you want without the overindulgence?

These recipes show you a few ways to satisfy your sweet tooth without loading up the calories.

By simply changing a few ingredients typically found in desserts for something equally tasty but less calorific, these delicious sweet treats will round off any meal, guilt-free...

Chocolate and Clementine Mousse

Cacao and cocoa powder are rich sources of magnesium, which is essential for many functions in the body including bone and heart health.

....

Ingredients

- 2 tsp extra virgin coconut oil
- 1 medium avocado, peeled and stoned
- 2 tbsp raw cacao or cocoa powder
- 1 tbsp honey
- 1 clementine, peeled and cut into thin slices

Method

1. Melt the coconut oil by placing it in a small bowl over hot water.

2. Reserving a couple of clementine slices, put all the other ingredients into a food processor and blend until thick and smooth.

3. Spoon the mixture into two bowls and chill in the refrigerator. The mousse will keep well for a few hours in the fridge, so can be prepared in advance.

4. Decorate with slices of clementine and serve.

....

Preparation: 6 mins

Raw Cacao and Banana Mousse

This pudding is not only free from dairy and refined sugar, but it is also very nutrient-rich, providing more than one-third of your daily intake of magnesium, iron and vitamin B6.

Ingredients

- 2 medium very ripe bananas, peeled
- 1 medium very ripe avocado, halved, stoned and flesh scooped out
- 1 tsp cashew nut butter
- 4 tbsp raw cacao powder or cocoa powder
- Pinch of salt
- 1 tbsp extra virgin coconut oil
- 80g raspberries (fresh or frozen)

Preparation: 25 mins

Method

1. Place all of the ingredients except the raspberries into a food processor and blend until completely smooth. You can also use a bowl and stick blender. Once blended, spoon into bowls and leave in the refrigerator for 20 minutes.

2. In a small bowl, lightly crush half of the raspberries, then add the rest of the raspberries and mix.

3. Serve the chilled mousse with the raspberry crush.

Energy: **325 kcals** Protein: **8.1g** Carbohydrate: **30.6g** Of which sugars: **23g** Fat: **20.1g** Of which saturates: **8.1g** Fibre: **8.4g** Salt: **0.6g**

Baked Banana with Coconut

Bananas are high in vitamin B6, which converts food into energy. They are also high in the electrolyte potassium, making them a perfect snack after or during exercise.

Ingredients

- 2 large bananas, sliced in half lengthways
- 25g desiccated coconut
- 2 tsp honey

Preparation: 5 mins
Cooking: 10 mins

Method

1. Preheat the oven to 200°C / gas mark 6.
2. Place the bananas on a small baking tray lined with foil. Sprinkle with the coconut and drizzle the honey evenly over the bananas, then gather up the corners of the foil to create a parcel.
3. Place the baking tray with the parcel in the oven and bake for approximately 10 minutes. Be careful of steam when opening the parcel.
4. Serve warm.

Energy: **213 kcals** Protein: **2.2g** Carbohydrate: **34.8g** Of which sugars: **32g** Fat: **8.1g**
Of which saturates: **6.8g** Fibre: **4.1g** Salt: **0.0g**

Oaty Blackberry and Apple Crumble

Blackberries and oranges are very good sources of vitamin C, which is important for many body processes, including healthy skin and connective tissues, and a strong immune system. A serving of this crumble provides one-third of your recommended daily intake of vitamin C.

Ingredients

For the topping:
- 50g wholemeal plain flour
- 50g oats
- Pinch of allspice
- 25g light muscovado sugar
- 2 tbsp butter, cold and cut into small pieces (plus a little more for greasing)

For the filling:
- 100g blackberries (fresh or frozen)
- 170g cooking apple, peeled, cored and thinly sliced
- 3 tbsp orange juice

Preparation: 15 mins
Cooking: 30 mins

Method

1. Preheat the oven to 180°C / gas mark 4.
2. Lightly grease a medium ovenproof dish.
3. Mix the flour, oats, allspice and sugar together in a bowl.
4. Rub in the butter until the mixture looks like breadcrumbs.
5. In a separate bowl, mix the blackberries, apple and orange juice together, then tip into the ovenproof dish, evenly spreading out the fruit mixture.
6. Sprinkle the crumble mixture over the fruit.
7. Bake for 30 minutes until the fruit has softened and the crumble is crisp.

Energy: **405 kcals** Protein: **6.9g** Carbohydrate: **62.4g** Of which sugars: **30.6g** Fat: **15.4g**
Of which saturates: **8.8g** Fibre: **8.7g** Salt: **0.3g**

Apricot Fool

A portion of dried fruit is 40g which means this dessert counts as one of your five-a-day.

Ingredients

- 12 dried apricots
- 10g sunflower, flax or pumpkin seeds
- 150g low fat vegetarian cream cheese
- 1 tsp honey
- 10g toasted flaked almonds

Preparation: 10 mins
Cooking: 20 mins

Method

1. Place the apricots in a small pan with just enough hot water to cover them, and simmer on a low heat for about 20 minutes until the apricots have softened and the water has reduced to a syrup.

2. While the apricots are cooking, grind the seeds using a pestle and mortar or a small blender.

3. Once the apricots have finished cooking, allow them to cool a bit before blending them and their syrup into a thick purée with a stick blender.

4. In a bowl combine the cream cheese, honey and apricot purée, stirring until smooth.

5. Spoon the cream cheese and apricot mixture into two glasses, sprinkle with ground seeds and toasted almonds, and serve.

Energy: **307 kcals** Protein: **10.1g** Carbohydrate: **30.3g** Of which sugars: **27.5g** Fat: **17g**
Of which saturates: **7.4g** Fibre: **5g** Salt: **0.9g**

Warm Citrus Fruits with Toasted Coconut

Vitamin C can help your body to absorb more iron from plant-based sources like green vegetables, tofu and nuts, making this a great dessert option.

Ingredients

- 2 large grapefruits
- 2 medium oranges
- 1 tbsp brown sugar
- 1 tbsp unsalted butter
- 30g desiccated coconut
- 150g low fat Greek yogurt

Preparation: 10 mins
Cooking: 5 mins

Method

1. Preheat the grill to a high setting.
2. Remove the rind from the citrus fruits and slice each one into circles about 1cm thick.
3. Place the circles in a shallow baking dish, trying not to overlap them.
4. Sprinkle the sugar over the fruit and dot with butter. Grill the fruit until it turns golden, then sprinkle with coconut and grill again until the coconut is toasted.
5. Serve with yogurt.

Energy: **402 kcals** Protein: **9.7g** Carbohydrate: **56.8g** Of which sugars: **56.8g** Fat: **16.1g**
Of which saturates: **12.4g** Fibre: **13.8g** Salt: **0.3g**

Pineapple with Anise-Lime Syrup and Coconut

Pineapples contain an enzyme called bromelain which helps the body to digest protein. This is why pineapples are often regarded as a digestive aid.

Ingredients

- 1 x 300g can pineapple chunks in juice, drained, juice reserved
- 1 medium lime, juice and zest
- 1 star anise
- 1 tbsp desiccated coconut
- 2 heaped tbsp low fat Greek yogurt

Preparation: 5 mins
(plus 30 minutes
chilling time)
Cooking: 5 mins

Method

1. Put 2 tbsp of the juice from the pineapple in a small saucepan with the lime juice and zest and the star anise.
2. Bring to the boil and simmer for a few minutes until it has reduced a little. Turn off the heat and allow to infuse until cool.
3. Put the pineapple chunks in a bowl and add the cooled infused syrup. Place the bowl in the refrigerator, and allow the pineapple to marinate for 30 minutes.
4. Toast the coconut by placing it in a small frying pan over a low heat and moving it around for about 5 minutes until golden.
5. Spoon the marinated pineapple into small bowls, top with a dollop of yogurt and sprinkle with the toasted coconut.

Energy: **143 kcals** Protein: **3.2g** Carbohydrate: **22.3g** Of which sugars: **22.3g** Fat: **4.8g**
Of which saturates: **4.3g** Fibre: **2.4g** Salt: **0.1g**

Salted Chocolate and Prune Truffles

Raw cacao and cocoa powder are very rich sources of minerals, which makes these tasty treats not only delicious but also good for you.

Ingredients

- 100g prunes, pitted
- 50g ground almonds
- 1½ tbsp raw cacao or cocoa powder (plus a little more for dusting)
- Pinch of salt
- 2 whole almonds

Method

1. Put the prunes in a bowl, cover with boiling water and leave to soak for 20 minutes until soft.

2. Drain the prunes and place them in a food processor along with the ground almonds, cacao powder and a pinch of salt.

3. Blend the mixture until it resembles a soft dough then transfer it from the processor onto a plate.

4. Divide the mixture into four. Carefully cut each whole almond into two and encase each half almond with the mixture and roll into balls.

5. Dust with a little cacao powder and serve.

Preparation: 20 mins

Baked Apples with Raisins

Apples contain pectin which is a soluble fibre that helps lower cholesterol.

....

Ingredients

- 2 medium cooking apples, cored
- 30g raisins
- 2 tsp honey
- 1 tsp cinnamon
- 10g butter

Method

1. Preheat the oven to 180°C / gas mark 4.

2. In a small bowl, combine the raisins with the honey and cinnamon, then stuff each apple with the mixture.

3. Top each apple with a little butter.

4. Stand apples on a lined baking sheet and bake for about 45 minutes until softened.

5. Serve warm.

....

Energy: **176 kcals** Protein: **1.0g** Carbohydrate: **35.4g** Of which sugars: **35.4g** Fat: **4.4g**
Of which saturates: **2.6g** Fibre: **4.3g** Salt: **0.1g**

Preparation: 5 mins
Cooking: 45 mins

Recipes in alphabetical order

Notes: